Writing Workshop

A Manual for College ESL Writers

Stephanie Coffin and Barbara Hall
Georgia Perimeter College

Illustrations by Tom Ferguson

The McGraw-Hill Companies, Inc.
Primis Custom Publishing

New York St. Louis San Francisco Auckland Bogotá
Caracas Lisbon London Madrid Mexico Milan Montreal
New Delhi Paris San Juan Singapore Sydney Tokyo Toronto

McGraw·Hill
A Division of The McGraw·Hill Companies

Writing Workshop
A Manual for College ESL Writers

McGraw-Hill's Primis Custom Series consists of products that are produced from camera-ready copy. Peer review, class testing, and accuracy are primarily the responsibility of the author(s).

7 8 9 0   QSR QSR   0 9 8 7 6 5 4

ISBN 0-07-228753-5

Editor: Judy Ice
Cover Design: Victoria Bacher
Printer/Binder: Quebecor Printing Dubuque, Inc.

Table of Contents

Acknowledgments

Many people have helped us produce this manual. Dr. Charles Schroen, director of the ESL program at Georgia Perimeter College, and Ms. Helen Boothe, our departmental secretary, made it possible to field-test an earlier draft in our composition classes. Many thanks to them. We thank our colleagues Tim Brotherton for field-testing and Roland Cassie for both field-testing and carefully editing the earlier draft. Pam Suskauer, a colleague teaching in the American Language Program at the University of Georgia, provided invaluable advice and commentary. We thank our other colleagues in the ESL Department for their considerable support in this project.

Special thanks goes to Tom Ferguson, the fine and funny artist who provides the delightful illustrations of what may otherwise be dry grammar; to Wenji Zou, whose lettering and line drawings grace these pages; and to all of our ESL students, especially those who so willingly gave us their writing to use in this text.

Finally we thank those close to us: Tom Coffin, who provided technical and editing assistance throughout the writing of this manual; David Marcus, who also gave freely his editing skills and his knowledge and ideas about writing and grammar; and Simon Coffin, for his elegant cover design. We'll bake y'all some cookies!

Stephanie Coffin and Barbara Hall
Georgia Perimeter College
555 North Indian Creek Dr.
Clarkston, Georgia 30021-2396

To the Instructor

Writing Workshop is a writing and editing text for college level and college-bound ESL students. It may also be very useful for EFL students in intensive language courses. This manual includes the following distinctive features:

* an easy-to-use analytical chart contrasting English with six other languages
* a uniform approach to error hierarchy and editing strategies
* samples of student writing illustrate the discussion on the parts of an essay
* student essays used for analytical exercises
* focus on explanation and application of grammar
* perforated pages for a "user-friendly" workbook style

APPROACH

Writing Workshop reflects our combined 20 years of teaching at-risk college ESL students. These students were assigned to the English as a Second Language (ESL) program at DeKalb College (now Georgia Perimeter College) after failing the writing test for entrance into freshman composition classes. We emphasize the acquisition of self-editing tools and techniques that help students became stronger, more independent writers. In addition, we present students with many peer writing samples to read, critique, and edit, allowing them to recognize that their language problems may not be unique or even personal.

We have found it difficult to find grammar and writing texts appropriate for college-level ESL classes. Some texts treat all grammar errors with equal emphasis with little regard for special needs. Others do not adequately treat those particularly problematic areas of grammar, such as prepositions and articles, that most affect our students. We believe that our treatment of grammar will help to fill a significant gap in ESL textbooks.

DESIGN

Writing Workshop begins with **Parts of the Essay.** We explain how to write "hooks," body paragraphs, and conclusions, using student writing as examples and models. **Editing,** the next section, encourages a uniform approach to error hierarchy and editing strategies and priorities. This section includes standardized marking symbols for instructors to use, an error correction sheet with instructions for use, and a useful record sheet for errors of in-class compositions. The center section, **Grammar and Exercises,** breaks down the traditional separation of grammar and writing by concentrating on the major errors occurring in actual student writing, both in the examples and, particularly, in the writing produced by the student him- or herself. **Student Writing Samples and Exercises** contains a range of student papers that represent what students actually produce in college ESL classes. In **Writing Topics and Assignments** we suggest practice writing topics and include several writing assignments for out-of-class work.

To the Student

This manual is intended to augment and help systematize your efforts to prepare for college-level composition classes in English. Its front-to-back order is logical, but arbitrary. Your writing, from timed in-class essays to literary response papers done at home, and your particular writing needs should determine how you and your instructor order and use the book

How does *Writing Workshop* differ from other ESL textbooks?

* **Parts of the Essay:** The manual guides you through those parts of the essay that have proven to be the most difficult for our students. For example, we provide 13 different suggestions to start your paper in the "Hooks" section, accompanied with sample "hooks" and introductions written by ESL students . The sections on Body Paragraph Development and suggestions for Conclusions follow this pattern.

* **Editing:** We suggest tested methods for you and your instructor to determine your particular pattern (or patterns) of grammar errors in written English. You are encouraged to maintain an error record sheet to help you reduce your mistakes in later writing.

* **Focus on Grammar:** Good writing and good grammar are inseparable. The Grammar section concentrates on the major grammatical errors that second-language students tend to make as they learn English. It encourages you to think about the specific errors you make in your own writing. It seeks to deepen your understanding of the impact of your first language, both negative and positive, on your use of English. Grammar rules are presented and explained in simple language that allows you to "make sense" out of English. We include exercises that encourage you to take responsibility for the grammar you are learning through active participation and practice.

* **Student Writing:** The writing samples we use are by students, not published authors or famous people. We want to show some of the range of writing that students produce in advanced ESL composition courses. These student essays may not represent the most beautiful or elegant prose that exists in our language, but we know from experience the value of presenting achievable models for students to learn from. Of course, you are also encouraged to read and study fine writing by more experienced writers.

* **Language Comparisons:** If your first language is Arabic, Chinese, Japanese, Korean, Spanish, or Vietnamese, we recommend that you compare your language to English in the language chart on the following page. We also recommend that you study the list of predicted errors that speakers of your language tend to make in English.

This manual reflects our combined 20 years working with ESL students to overcome their difficulties mastering the elements necessary for college-level composition in English. We hope that you find it useful.

A Contrastive Look at the Grammar of Six Languages – English

Language	Word Order	Word Form	Verb System	Nouns and Articles	Plurals	Other	Predicted Errors for Native speakers
English	SVO rigid word order; adj before nouns; right branching relative clauses	prefixes and suffixes – both derivational (ex. *ness, ist*) and inflectional (*s, 's, ing, ed, er, est*)	extensive tense and aspect with auxiliary verbs and modals; wide use of passive voice	count and non-count; indefinite and definite articles in complex system	pl nouns marked with "s"; some demonstra- tive adj noun agree	alphabetic; inconsistant spelling due to infusion of other languages	agree, verb tense, verb form, and sent structure

Some features of the English language:
1. SVO strict word order with few exceptions
2. Complex tense system
3. Borrowings from other languages
4. Complex system of articles
5. Redundancy in plural/sing features

Key To Abbreviations:

s = subject

v = verb

o = object

masc = masculine

fem = feminine

left-branching = adjective clause branches to the left of the noun

right branching = adjective clause branches to the right of the noun

tonal = different sounds of the same letter depict different meanings

inflecting = changes from endings on words that either indicate grammatical function, create new words or change grammatical category

wf = word form

wo = word order

pl = plural

adv. = adverb

agree =agreement

adj = adjective

aux = auxiliary

poss = possesive

A Contrastive Look at the Grammar of Six Languages

Language	Word Order	Word Form	Verb System	Nouns and Articles	Plurals	Other	Predicted Errors
Arabic	VSO (formal); SVO; VO; adv many possible positions; adj follow nouns	all verbs, nouns, adj, participles formed from 3-consonant roots, modify by simple prefix, suffix, and infix	past, present, future and some perfect tenses; no "be" in the present; S (pro) + V combined in verb	definite articles; no indefinite articles; nouns are masc. or fem.	nouns marked; agree rules different	alphabetic right to left writing; no fixed punct rules	spelling, punctuation, verb forms, tenses, agree, number, and indefinite articles
Chinese	SVO; all noun modifiers before nouns; English post modifiers problematic; adv comes before v and adj	non-inflecting	uses adverbials; wo and context; different concept of time; "be" often dropped; no auxiliaries; modals not similar	no articles; count/non-count not similar in Chinese	plurality is rare	non-alphabetic; tonal	wo, wf, parallelism, verb tense, verb form, agree, number, and articles
Japanese	SOV; left branching relative clauses	nouns can also function as adj and adv	verb contains S and O; no "be"; passive used in a different way; no modals	no articles; no distinction between count and non-count	nouns not marked	respect/formal language; many English words in lexicon	wo, wf, parallelism, verb tense, verb form, agree, number, articles, and prepositions

Language	Word Order	Word Form	Verb System	Nouns and Articles	Plurals	Other	Predicted Errors
Korean	SOV; right branch relative clause; adj before noun	particles (added to nouns, verbs, adverbs and sent end) mark S, O, emphasis, contrast, conjunctive and sentence; suffixes on nouns, verbs, adj, and adv	verb stem + any of 5 elements: voice, honorific, tense, humble, or inflectional ending; stem and inflectional necessary; both suffix and aux	no articles	pl element focuses on individual items in a group, esp people not animals or things; if noun quantified, pl not added; plural is non-commital	alphabetic; honorific suffixes and vocabulary	wf, verb tense, verb form, agree, number, articles, and prepositions
Spanish	SVO and VSO and V; adv many possible positions; adj follows nouns	suffixes; inflections on adj, poss, nouns; verb tenses change form; conjugation for all persons	range of tenses and composite forms; verbs have endings; passive voice; S (pron) + V combined	masc/ fem article; definite article has wider use	articles, adj, possess. as well as nouns are pl or sing	all nouns and art + poss adj are masc/fem; many English cognates	sentence structure, missing subjects, word order, and word form
Vietnamese	SVO; right branch relative clause; no "it is, there is"; adj follows noun	mono-syllabic; non-inflecting	"be" verb rare; tense and aspect expressed using context and time words; passive is rare	no parallels in English; system of classifiers, such as "this" and "one"	quantified by adjectives; no indicator of plural on nouns	6 tones; alphabetic	wf, parallelism, verb tense, verb form, agreement, number, and articles

Language Questionnaire

Take time to complete this language questionnaire. By analyzing the grammar of your own language, you will be able to recognize many of the areas of difficulty when you write in English.

1. What is your first language?

2. Do you write in your first language?

3. Have you studied the grammar of your first language?

4. Have you ever written an essay in your first language?

5. Does writing in your first language go from left to right? Right to left? Top to bottom?

6. Does writing in your first language contain marks of punctuation like periods, commas, or semicolons? If so, which ones?

7. How does your first language writing include breaks for paragraphs?

8. What is the basic sentence structure of your language? (SVO; SOV; VSO)

9. Do verbs in your language have endings that indicate time? If not, how does your language indicate time?

10. Do nouns in your language show singularity or plurality? If so, how?

11. Does your language have a system of articles? If so, how does it work?

12. Does your language use prepositions? Are they before or after nouns?

13. Where are adjectives placed in sentences? Are they before or after nouns?

14. Are adverbs placed in a fixed order in sentences in your language or can they be positioned in different places?

15. What features does your first language have that English does not have? (honorific pronouns or vocabulary? diacritical marks? tones?)

16. What areas of English grammar do you consider your weakest?

Section One:
Parts of the Essay

Parts of the Essay

The parts of an essay are often compared to the parts of a hamburger! The top bun which is puffy and round has the hook and the thesis. Like a hamburger, this is the part that you see first. The insides of the hamburger with its variety of meat, (or meat substitute), cheese, and all the condiments including lettuce, tomato, onions, mustard, catsup, and mayonnaise, reflect the variety of the support inside the body paragraphs. The conclusion is like the top bun, but thinner. Like the conclusion the bottom bun creates the boundary of the essay and finishes the essay.

Other people compare the essay structure to the body of a person. The head (introductory paragraph) gives the body and conclusion the direction and shape. The body (body paragraphs) fills in the essay with details. Finally, the feet conclude the essay and provide a grounding. Whichever image you prefer, the essay must follow these general parameters.

Introduction: The hook attracts and interests the reader. The thesis: provides the reader with a plan or indicates what the essay will be about.

Body Paragraphs: The body paragraphs provide support for the thesis. They fill in the essay with details, examples, descriptions, opinions, and facts.

Conclusion: The conclusion gives the essay a sense of closure.

Things to remember:

1. Every paragraph must have at least three sentences. The typical paragraph ranges from 5-8 sentences, but a more developed paragraph may contain 10-12 sentences.

2. You don't have to write the essay beginning with the introduction and proceeding to the conclusion. Many students find it easier to write the body paragraphs first! Experiment with what is easiest for you. Writing is discovery. Your ideas may change as you write.

Writing Hooks:

One Two, Many Hooks

The introductory paragraph is often the hardest paragraph to write. It consists of two parts: the hook and the thesis. The purpose of a hook is to attract and draw the reader into the writing. It is similar to a "first impression." If a hook is exciting, the reader continues to read. If the hook is boring, the reader is likely to find something else to read or something else to do.

Here are a number of specific techniques that good writers use to create interesting hooks to begin their essays. Following the description of each hook is an example written by an ESL writer.

After you have read over a sample of the hooks below, practice writing different hooks for your essays. This practice will give you flexibility. Hooks are used in all types of writing, from newspaper articles to journal writing and even scientific writing. Notice the kinds of hooks that other writers use.

1. *Questions: Ask one or more questions to arouse your reader's curiosity and to alert him or her to the subject matter of your essay.*

Are you curious about Chinese Kung-Fu? Do you believe in the power of those supermen who demonstrate Kung-Fu in the movies? Is Chinese Kung-Fu just a form of external fighting skills?

2. *Anecdote: Begin with an anecdote. An anecdote is a short story about a personal experience that is designed to make your reader empathize with the writer or the topic. It could be sad, humorous, or shocking.*

A few days ago, we were walking down Piedmont Avenue, close to Piedmont Park. Suddenly we saw a man who seemed to want to talk to us. We did not pay attention to his behavior and kept on walking. However, he approached us and started speaking. As soon as he found out our Colombian nationality, he exclaimed, "You come from the land of cocaine and marijuana!" As we are proud of being from Colombia, we felt obligated to defend our country. He was friendly, so we did not get mad but tried to explain the truth. "We have never used that stuff. We don't even know what it looks like. We have never dealt with it in our whole lives." He just laughed.

3. *Funnel: Provide historical or substantial information, beginning with a broad generalization and progressing to more specific information. This is called the funnel-type introduction, with the general information corresponding to the top, or widest part, of a funnel and the specific information corresponding to the bottom, or narrowest part, of a funnel. A funnel takes a wide stream and directs it to a specific place, and this type of introduction seizes the reader's thoughts and channels them toward a specific point.*

There are twelve national holidays in Japan. Most of these holidays are quite different from those of other countries because they originate in traditional Japanese ceremonies. However, the way people celebrate the New Year holidays in Japan is very similar to the way the Christmas holidays are celebrated in Christian countries. The New Year holidays, which are celebrated during the first three days of January, are the most exciting and important holidays of the year because they represent the beginning of the New Year. The Japanese people think that decisions made on New Year's Day bring them a successful year.

4. *Reverse-funnel: An alternate form of the funnel is the reverse funnel introduction in which the writer begins with specific data and proceeds to a generalization. This is an effective way to make the reader begin thinking analytically, to get him or her to try to understand why the specific facts or examples are related.*

Melody: That was her name. She had a beautiful face with blond hair which we thought matched her features well. She was also sweet and quite gentle. Altogether, she was perfect! No, we are not talking about a girl on TV, competing for a beauty title. Melody Frend was a perfect lady whom we interviewed at the Jimmy Carter Presidential Library. She was one of the archivists there, and she was assigned to be our guiding light as we explored the library.

5. *Unclear referent: Use pronouns in your first sentences but don't identify their referents until later in the paragraph or even in a subsequent paragraph.*

He graduated from college with honors. He helps me with my homework when I have difficult problems with algebra. He makes it very simple when he solves the problem, so I can easily get an "A" in my algebra test. He likes to help the homeless, and his favorite hobby is collecting stamps. He loves to play tennis. He is my oldest brother Chun Soo Kim. The best advice I ever received from my oldest brother was to be honest and to stay in school.
                                                                    – Sung Soo Kim

6. *Definition: Define your topic, either in your own words or with a direct quotation from a dictionary. This is particularly useful if a key word in your topic is abstract. Be sure to credit the dictionary.*

Longman Dictionary of Contemporary English defines education as the "process by which a person's mind and character are developed through teaching, especially through formal instruction at a school or college." It is not necessary for everybody to finish college. However, now at the time of knowledge and computers, more and more people understand that in order to be useful in our society, we need to be more educated. Therefore, in order to learn professional skills many people go to college.

– Raisa Feldman

7. **Physical Description:** *Use a physical description to set a scene.*

Imagine a river flowing gently. It is twilight, and the air is cool and fresh. On the river are thousands of lights from candles floating in miniature boats, and the delicate scent of fresh flowers drifts across the water. This is the *Loy Kratona* in my native Thailand.

8. **Mood:** *Create a mood by describing an emotional frame of reference.*

It was 7:00 p.m. when my shivering finger pushed on the doorbell button of the Sarts family home. Just before the door was opened, I checked myself to make sure my hair was not messy, my new shirt fit uniformly into my belt, and my pants did not have any wrinkles or spots. "Everything is right," I thought as the door opened and the warm, wide smile of Mrs. Sarts invited me in to my first American dinner and to something else.

9. **News flash:** *Give your writing a sense of immediacy by stating the exact date, time and location of the event you will describe.*

April 30, 1975, was the day that North Vietnam took over South Vietnam. Just one week before that, my family and I were floating on a small boat out to the ocean, trying to look for the American ships.

10. **Flashback:** *Begin writing as if you are planning to tell about a present event, but then refer to some memory of a past event to reminisce about or to illustrate your topic. This technique is called flashback, and it is used as a way to move your reader from the present time to some past moment.*

While I was sitting in my bedroom, my eyes wandered into another time period. My wanderings ended when I saw myself twelve years ago without any shirt on. I saw my whole family on a small boat getting ready to leave Vietnam. I remember that I was supposed to stay in Vietnam with my uncle. I saw myself being so scared and anxious. I felt like reaching my hands out and pulling up my whole family. As I looked at my family, my tears fell. I can imagine how much pain it was for my parents to drag along eight children. Because of this passage, I consider my family very different from other families.

– Linh Nguyen

11. **Common Ground:** *Make a statement that your reader can identify with, to establish common ground on which the two of you (writer and reader) can communicate. This is the most common and overused introduction. It requires the least thought and does little to encourage your reader to continue. Try to think of a better hook than this one.*

> Like most people everywhere, I love holidays. I plan how I'll spend them for months, putting red marks on my calendar and sometimes chuckling to myself as the time draws near.

12. **Authority:** *Quote an authority or well-known figure and analyze the implications of that quotation. This hook is often used with research papers. It is difficult to use in timed writings, but you might be able to remember a quotation that would fit your essay.*

13. **Statistics:** *Use statistical data to hook your reader and startle him or her into paying attention. Like the preceding hook, the use of statistics as a hook is usually used in research and papers where the student has time to gather information. However, it is very effective if you know statistics about the subject that you are writing about.*

Exercise 1: *Read the following hooks and identify them using the samples above. Notice where the hook shifts to thesis. Underline the thesis.*

A.   In winter morning, I was really reluctant to get out of my car. I preferred sitting in my warm car to enjoy looking at the different vivid colors of the maple trees. How fresh looking the student parking lot was. Slowly, the maple leaves dropped down while the winds were blowing. Then I walked toward my class. Suddenly I felt like walking and feet felt like they were stepping on a wild and soft blanket. The maple trees reminded me of my country which does not have maple trees, so I unconsciously imagined what I was doing in Vietnam. If I were to move back to my country, I thought my life would be like a free bird to take a trip around the country, and I would find a job and continue my bachelor's degree for four years.

                                                                    – Kieu Sen

Type of Hook:_____

B.   August 20, 1975, I was born in a small town called Tacloban in the Phillippines. When I was eight years old, my mom married an American man who worked in the Air Force. He was a great stepdad. On my 11th birthday, my stepdad asked my mother and me to live with him in America. I was happy because I would finally live in the U.S. I remembered the first time I arrived in Georgia. It was cold and windy. We arrived two days before Halloween. My stepdad took my to Honey Creek Elementary School. I was nervous because I did not know how to speak English. I had to go in order to continue my education. This is where I began to learn about the major differences between English and my first language.

                                                                    – Adelfa Luceriano

Type of Hook: _____

Writing the Thesis:

The Thesis Statement

Just as the topic sentence controls the paragraph, the thesis statement serves to control the essay. The thesis statement has two important functions. It states the main idea of the essay, and it suggests the organizational plan of the essay.

A good thesis has the following features:

1. It is a complete sentence, not a question.

2. It contains the writer's opinion and does not simply state a fact.

3. It restricts or limits a broad topic to something that can be covered in a multi-paragraph composition.

4. It may suggest the essay's overall organizational plan, though it should not give "stage directions" (i.e., "I am going to write about my adjustments to college").

Exercise 2: *Read the following thesis statements. Evaluate each one of them as G for Good, F for Fair, or U for Unacceptable and state why.*

_____ 1. Watching television is a waste of time.

_____ 2. Why are most Americans finding it impossible to diet?

_____ 3. I am going to write about some cultural differences between the U.S. and Korea.

_____ 4. Learning a second language as an adult can be both frustrating and stimulating.

_____ 5. American colleges compared to European colleges.

_____ 6. My sister and my mother are alike in many ways, especially in manners and values.

_____ 7. Cartagena, Colombia is a center for tourism all year round.

_____ 8. I prefer the semester system in college over the quarter system.

_____ 9. The adjustments I have made by living in the United States for the last five years have made me a strong and more aggressive person.

_____ 10. The importance of writing classes in college.

Developing Body Paragraphs:

Body Paragraphs:
Common Kinds of Support

The kind of support that you use in your essay generally depends on your thesis and the kind of essay you are writing. The following paragraphs exemplify some common types of support for essays. Sometimes paragraphs are a combination of these kinds of support and not simply one kind.

1. **Examples in the body paragraph:** *the writer uses single items that serve as models or samples; examples may be from the writer's own experience or from others; one example may be discussed in depth, as in an "extended" example.*

In Iman Foufa's essay (Sample Eight), she uses five separate examples of movies that she likes. In the second body paragraph she discusses three of these examples:

After having lost all hope of being in love again, she saw him, and they knew that that was it. They knew that they were born for each other. I love these romantic movies because they give me a moment of dream, of hope that some day it is going to happen to me. Romance is so beautiful and so sad at the same time, and I like that because love without suffering is too boring. For example, *Legends of the Fall* is so romantic that I saw it more than four times, and because all of their love was impossible, it was much more romantic and interesting. Indeed, the best movie I liked was *Don Juan*, the lover of every woman on earth. For the short time of the movie, I saw myself as a woman and being loved for that. Moreover, I really enjoy the stories in which people are forbidden from really enjoying their love and because of that, they get to know its real importance. I like movies where love is the winner at the end, as in *Dirty Dancing*, where after hard and beautiful times, the love of Patrick Swayze and Jennifer Grey finally won.

2. **Description in the body paragraph:** *the writer uses sensory details, such as sounds, smells, tastes, or colors, which serve to create images for the reader.*

In her essay, "The First Time I Lost Someone I Loved," Manuela Saramondi describes the bleakness of the hospital where her uncle was dying:

It was when my uncle was at the hospital that I realized the gravity of his sickness. He was there for a couple of months and had a room by himself. It was a white-grey room that gave me a sense of sadness everytime I entered and smelled the antiseptic white-washed floors. I felt sad not only because I knew Vito was sick with cancer, but also because the colors that were surrounding my uncle's life were sad. The blank white ceilings and grey curtains seemed unable to help his soul. I knew from his hazel eyes that he was very sad. After no improvement took place at the hospital, he and his wife decided to move him home.

3. **Narration in the body paragraph:** *the writer tells a story with attention to what happened in order of time, – a chronological ordering of events.*

This is a body paragraph from Adis Bojcic's essay "Life In and Out of Hell" where he chronologically narrates how his family was personally affected by the takeover of Bosnia by the Serbs:

In early March, when the Yugoslav People's Army (later known as the Serbian or Chetniks) started bringing extra tanks, armory, and personnel, the citizens thought it was just a military display. We said, "Maybe the politicians are just playing games; they are trying to scare us; they will not shoot. They will find the way out of the crisis peacefully." But in a few weeks, when the Army started locating the personnel and weaponry on the strategic hills around the city, we sensed the trouble. That was still not good enough to persuade the people to get their important things to a safe place. My parents acted normally, except they bought extra food and accessories for our house. We thought, "Even if the fighting starts, the Serbs would never be able to enter the city." Soon, the citizens tried to arm themselves, but it was too late. On the 4th of April, the Serbs took seventy percent of the country, and half of my city. Unfortunately, my house with all my pictures, clothes, and other belongings was on the "east" occupied side.

4. **Personal Opinion in the body paragraph:** *the writer discusses his/her opinion about a subject or another person's opinion which may be in support or in contrast.*

In Iman Foufa's essay, she gives the personal opinion of an Algerian male friend of hers on the topic of "Should a Married Woman Work?" Then she expresses her disagreement with his opinion.

Even though the question about whether women should work is not over today, some people still think that women should stay at home, take care of the house, and prepare the meals for the husband. For example, once I asked an Algerian friend of mine what he thinks about this subject, and he told me that he would expect his future wife to be a housewife since he can take care of the house finances alone. He thinks that there is no reason for his wife to work as much as he does, and this is the natural way in which responsibilities are divided in Algeria. When I asked him what he thinks about the possibility for him to stay home and for his wife to work, his only answer for that was, "This is against nature." However, I cannot figure out any reason why a woman should stay at home and get bored while the husband is working.

5. **Facts or Statistics in the body paragraph:** *the writer uses figures that can be proved or verified; often this requires some research and documentation.*

This example from a student's paper on the Korean writing system contains numerous facts that the student knows as common knowledge, and therefore no documentation is required.

The Korean writing system, created by Sejong, the fourth king of the Yi Dynasty, was designed so that the common and lower classes could read and write better. It was introduced in 1446 and called Han gul. Han gul was designed as an alphabet with 24 basic writing symbols. There are 14 consonants and 11 vowels. Although Han gul was created for the lower classes, now all Koreans are using this writing system today.

Exercise 3: *Read the following body paragraphs and identify what kind of support is being used. Note: Body paragraphs may contain several different kinds of support.*

A.   Before I started DeKalb College, I thought college would be as easy as having dinner. Especially, I thought I could succeed easily in math and writing. When I was in Vietnam, some friends sent me letters from California. They said that they were the best students in their Mathematics classes. They said that the college math level was the same as the high school level of my country. Some of them could win writing prizes, and their essays were published in books. They said that Vietnamese students studied more grammar than Americans. I trusted what they said. I thought they were reasonable. Because we always copied our lessons from blackboards when we studied, our writing grammar was more careful than the American students. I was so excited before I started college. I thought that I could easily be the best student in my math and writing class.

                                                                        – Kieu Sen

Kind of support: _____

B.   The Korean flag is called Taegegkee by Koreans, and it consists of Taegeeg in the middle of the flag and four stick shapes around it. The Taegeeg is in a round shape and is divided into two parts by red and blue colors. Each color means yin and yang which are the two basic principles of the universe in ancient philosophy. Yin is the female principle, characterized as dark and negative, and Yang is the male principle, characterized as light and positive. These two, yin and yang, are the principles that form the basis of the Korean flag. As the Korean flag stands for yin and yang, Korean people have the spirit of understanding the principles of the universe and the soul of living based on them.

                                                                        – Suyoung Choi

Kind of support:_____

Working with Transitions:

A Guide to Transitions

Transitions are used as bridges to help the reader stay with the writer. Use transitions at the beginning of the sentence, in the middle or at the end. Transitions are also used at the beginning, middle, and end of paragraphs. Transitions can be one word, a phrase or even a sentence. Transitions help your writing stay coherent, which means to read as a "whole" instead of as unconnected parts. Study the following transitions, so you can use them quickly and correctly.

Transitions that explain: *now, in addition, for, in this case, furthermore, in fact*

1. Now go two steps to the left and follow the hallway.
2. In addition there are 10 major colleges in the area.
3. The solution, in this case, is hard to figure out.
4. The conference went on for three days, in fact.

Transitions that emphasize: *certainly, indeed, above all, surely, most important*

1. Certainly taking the test was not fun.
2. Indeed, the salad of every meal is the course I enjoy.
3. Surely you agree that she is the tallest sister.
4. Above all, always check for errors even if the assignment is not an English assignment.
5. Most important, the tax form has to be in by April 1.

Transitions that qualify: *but, however, although, though, yet, except for*

1. The letter arrived two days after she had left, however.
2. We hoped, though, that she would not leave him after all.
3. Yet there was still a chance that she would come back.
4. Except for the essay question, I got all of them correct.

Transitions that illustrate: *for example, for instance, thus, such, next*

1. That solution, for example, is one that only a brilliant student could create.
2. For instance a telegram costs much more than a telephone call or a fax.
3. Next, think of registering early for any chemistry class you want to take.
4. Such an earthquake happens only once in a decade.
5. Thus my college career began in the Fall of 1993.

Transitions that add: *in addition, furthermore, also, moreover, first, second, third, etc., then*

1. In addition, the train stops in Decatur.
2. Furthermore, the time for registration is scheduled for day and evening students.
3. First, you include your money. Second, you include a self-addressed stamped envelope. Third, you put the correct address outside.
4. Then when you have finished, you drop the application in the mail.
5. The girls expected, moreover, to win an award for their efforts.

Transitions that compare: *like, in the same way, similarly, equally important, too*

1. Like most cats, dogs often sleep all day.
2. Similarly the Thai people enjoy curry in their food.
3. Equally important, the car needs to have the water checked along with the oil.

Transitions that contrast: *unlike, in contrast, whereas, on the other hand, instead*

1. Unlike winter fruit, the fruit in the summer comes from the local area.
2. On the other hand, it is nice to have someone to cook for you.
3. In contrast, the blue liquid does not turn color.
4. Instead the new law ended up costing the taxpayers more.

Transitions that concede: *although, nevertheless, of course, after all, clearly, still, yet*

1. She planned, nevertheless, to go ahead with the dinner.
2. After all, you can learn to write well if you want to.
3. Still it would be nice to go away for awhile.

Transitions that state a consequence: *therefore, as a result, consequently, accordingly, otherwise, so*

1. As a result, he had to pay the entire amount at one time.
2. Consequently, she ended up taking the class three times.
3. Accordingly, she telephones four companies for price estimates.

Transitions that sum up: *to sum up, finally, in conclusion, at last, in summary*

1. In conclusion, he ended his story with a bang.
2. At last, the end of the long quarter drew to a close.

Transitions of time: *meanwhile, at length, soon, afterward, during*
Transitions of place: *here, beyond, opposite to, nearby*

(Use commas after transitions at the beginning of the sentence if you want your reader to pause.)

Many transitions have only slight variations in meaning. If you are using a transition that you have never used before, check the dictionary for a written example of its particular use.

Oral Classroom Exercise: After everyone has studied the transition list and examples, a student should volunteer to begin a story. Each person in the class adds a sentence or two to the story AND a transition. Great fun. The challenge is for everyone to use a different transition each time.

Exercise 4: *Read over your last essay. Underline all your transitions. Consider if you could add more. Read over the list and try to "bridge" your ideas for the reader.*

Exercise 5: *Add transitions to the following story. Experiment with ones that you are not familiar with. Read your story after you have finished.*

The first day of college was quite an event for me. _____ when I went out to get into my car, it wouldn't start. _____ calling my friend to come get me, I _____ arrived. Here I was! It was my first day of college. _____ we couldn't find a parking place in one of the lots _____. We circled around and around while looking at the digital clock on the dashboard of the car. _____ my friend did not fill up his gas tank the night before, and the gas gauge was hovering around the big red empty indicator. _____ we found a spot. _____ we got out to begin looking for our classes, a big burly guy came and told us that we were in the visitor's parking lot. _____ we had to move. _____ when we finally arrived and found our first class, we were late. Both of us walked into the same class under the disapproving eyes of the teacher.

Ending the Essay:

Writing An Appropriate Conclusion

Most composition textbooks have plenty of suggestions about how to write introductions to essays, but few concrete suggestions about the endings of papers. Thus, many student writers get stuck at the end – in a rush and thinking that the only thing they can possibly do is to rewrite the thesis one more time. That, of course, is the solution only if your professor calls out, "Ten minutes left!" when you haven't even begun the conclusion, and you know that you need to save some time for editing.

In a short paper like an Exit exam or Timed Essay, however, a summary conclusion or thesis restatement is usually inappropriate. Your reader has read your paper in two or three minutes and probably has not forgotten its main ideas. Generally, a summary conclusion is used for a long work, a 10-page research paper or a 50-page master's thesis, but not for a 350 word composition. So, what other kinds of conclusions are possible?

1. **The Result:** *This type of conclusion naturally follows in a process or cause/effect paper in which you analyze the results of a process which you describe. This can also work for narrative papers in which you are describing a move or transition, and you want to end with what the situation is like now.*

   Here's an example of a **Result** conclusion from a narrative paper entitled "Failure" written by Chuck Sobezuk. In that paper, he describes how he learned a lesson from a day that he was accused of shoplifting some merchandise from Rich's Department Store:

   That day will always remain in my memory. I learned not to make the same mistake twice. I will never again get myself into a situation like that. Since that one day, I have never thought about taking something without paying for it.

2. **The Recommendation:** *A recommendation is often used as an ending when you have discussed a particular problem – perhaps the most serious problem in the US, or the problems that most ESL students face when they come from abroad. To suggest a solution reveals that you are going one step further in your analysis of the problem.*

   This is an example of a **Recommendation** conclusion from a paper entitled "School Comes First" where Ankur Desai argues that students, in particular high school students, should not work and go to school at the same time, if they can help it:

   In conclusion, teenagers shouldn't worry about working while in high school. Rather, they should concentrate on learning. Working at a job may seem fun and interesting in high school, but I would not recommend doing it. That job will be waiting for that person after the high school diploma is hanging on the wall!

3. **The Prediction:** *A prediction is a statement or hypothesis of something to happen in the future. The prediction might be personal — for example, what you might do in the future now that you have made the adaptation to American culture, or it might be a prediction for an entire culture, society, or institution.*

      This example of a **Prediction** conclusion is a personal prediction made by its writer, Adis Bojcic, at the end of his paper "Life In and Out of Hell," a paper that chronicles the escape of his family from the bloodshed of the Bosnian war:

      All of the things that happened in the war taught me a valuable lesson. From now on, I will have my documents ready for whatever happens. I will always try to do my best to see what is coming in the future, but look and observe from what is happening today. What has happened will not be forgotten. I will return one day to Bosnia, and then I will be ready to fight and to defend my homeland and family.

4. **The Quotation:** *Just as a quotation can be an interesting hook for an introduction, so can it serve to enhance your conclusion. The quotation doesn't necessarily have to be literary or scholarly, but can be a proverb from your country or a saying from your great uncle in China.*

      Here's an effective example of how a quotation can be used in an ending paragraph:

      All in all, my last seven years in the United States have changed me enormously, and I certainly found out how Americanized I had become when I returned to Korea in April 1997. Who was it who said, "You can never go home again"? That quotation certainly became true for me, as I sadly realized that I was no longer 100% Korean in dress, in language, and in culture.

5. **The "So What?" Ending:** *Oftentimes when you get stuck as a writer, simply ask the question: "So, what?" Why does this subject that I am writing about matter at all? What sort of broader picture does it fit into? This often helps get you started thinking about an ending.*

In this conclusion to a paper about a generation clash, Iman Foufa contrasts her traditional Algerian mother's view of the restricted life of a girl and woman with her own, more modern view. At the end, she philosophizes about a cultural change for Algerians:

Even though I was raised in Algeria, the country that I love the most in this world and am very proud of, I am very skeptical about some points that my culture let my mother believe in. In fact, I think that the twentieth century has revolutionized equal rights between men and women. It seems that now we, in Algeria, should be more worried about issues that are more important in the world than thinking about what a girl should do or not do in public.

Exercise 6: *Read the following conclusions and define what kind of conclusion is used by the writer.*

A.   In brief, I don't feel anxious when I have a challenge waiting for me. I would like to face any difficult situation that I have. Indeed, I think this attitude has helped me to survive and to flourish very well in America. I will keep this attitude to help me to be a successful person, and I will tell my children this experience and teach them my attitude.

– Herrick Ding

Kind of Conclusion: _____

B.   Consequently, I am doing very well in most of my courses in school, and also in managing the pocket allowance my father gave to me. These are the qualities that my father sat down and taught me when I was twelve years old. I am very grateful for them, for they have helped me to survive here.

– Ghamoti Anye Angwafo

Kind of Conclusion: _____

Some general guidelines for a conclusion:

1. Have one! Don't skip this part of the essay.
2. Avoid restating your thesis in the exact same words.
3. Avoid a direct summary of your main points in a short paper.
4. Avoid introducing any new topic or idea that causes the reader to lose track of your focus.

Section Two: Editing

Writing in my native language is hard because it is an art. Usually my Spanish teachers encouraged me to write as Cervantes. Cervantes means the same for Spanish speakers as Shakespeare for English speakers. However, writing in English is completely different. When I wrote all the essays for this class, I have learned more than I expected. There are two points that helped me: editing the essays and focusing on common errors.

The first is the use of editing essays. I used to write and type my essay at the same time. Now I take time for editing the essay. This tool is helping me a lot.

The second point is the use of focusing on common mistakes. Before I did not notice what were my common mistakes. Now I know what they are, and I try to find them on my essays.

In conclusion this class has helped me with my writing skills in English. Although I still do not write like an American person, the American people can understand my writing better.

– Olga L.

A Hierarchy of Grammar Errors and Symbols

Symbol		**Major Errors**

Symbol

FRAG

R-O

C-S

VF

VT

AGR

NUM

Major Errors

1. Sentence Structure Errors

Fragment: missing a subject, a verb, or the sentence is incomplete.
Incorrect: Because I went to the city to buy a heater for my car.
Correct: Because I went to the city to buy a heater for my car, I was late.

Run-on: two independent clauses put together with no punctuation and/or coordinator.
Incorrect: The boy ran out into the street he almost got hit by a car.
Correct: The boy ran out into the street, and he almost got hit by a car.

Comma Splice: two independent clauses put together with a comma.
Incorrect: We went to the mountains, we were late to the music festival.
Correct: We went to the mountains; however, we were late to the festival.

2. Verb Errors

Verb Form: the wrong form of the verb is used.
Incorrect: The children were laugh at the party.
Correct: The children were laughing at the party.

Verb Tense: the wrong tense is used in the context of the sentence or the paragraph.
Incorrect: I was in Atlanta since 1972.
Correct: I have been in Atlanta since 1972.

3. Agreement and Number Errors: the "s" is left off of nouns or verbs.

Agreement: subject/verb agreement rules are not followed.
Incorrect: John sit in the chair in front of the blackboard.
Correct: John sits in the chair in front of the blackboard.

Number: an "s" is not put on a noun to indicate plurality or is put on where it is not needed. Nouns and pronouns disagree.
Incorrect: I saw many car.
Correct: I saw many cars.

Incorrect: Most childrens go to school.
Correct: Most children go to school.

Symbol	
WF	

Serious Errors

4. Word Form Errors: a suffix is left off a word, or the wrong part of speech is used.

Incorrect:: The student was the smart in the class.
Correct: The student was the smartest in the class.

5. Word Choice Errors: a word is incorrectly used. Often a preposition is used incorrectly.

Incorrect: The student requested an application to the Administration Office.
Correct: The student requested an application from the Administration Office.
Incorrect: I take my coffee in the morning.
Correct: I drink my coffee in the morning.

6. Word Order Errors: words are put in the wrong order.

Incorrect: I wondered where does the boy live.
Correct: I wondered where the boy lives.

7. Article Errors: an article is left out, put in when not needed, or the wrong article is used.

Incorrect: The man who got on bus was wearing red hat.
Correct: The man who got on the bus was wearing a red hat.

Mechanical Errors

8. Spelling: a word is misspelled.

Incorrect: I drove to Ohio without stoping.
Correct: I drove to Ohio without stopping.

9. Punctuation: punctuation is put in when not needed, used incorrectly, or left out.

Incorrect: When you go to school let me know.
Correct: When you go to school, let me know.

10. Capitalization: a word is not capitalized when needed or unnecessarily capitalized.

Incorrect: I am learning english right now, but I want to learn french.
Correct: I am learning English right now, but I want to learn French.

Another Error

Non-English: this error describes writing that is not clear to the reader. It usually occurs when the writer is translating word-for-word from another language. It is the most serious error of all because usually the reader can't understand what the writer is trying to say.

Note: The Hierarchy of Errors is modeled after "The Twelve Common Problems Areas" from *Improving the Grammar of Written English* (1989) by Bevererly Benson and Patricia Byrd.

The symbols in the left column, from top to bottom, are:

WF

WC (PREP)

WO

ART

SP

P

CAP

NON. ENG

Exercise 7: *Use the **Hierarchy of Errors** and identify the error in each sentence. Write the name of the error beside each sentence. Work quickly. Skip the ones you can't figure out and come back to them.*

_____ 1. An automobile is a neccessary form of transportation in Atlanta.

_____ 2. He is taking math, english and u.s history.

_____ 3. Stop. Don't touch that hot burner.

_____ 4. There is island near my home.

_____ 5. The man which lives next door is a teacher.

_____ 6. This food is deliciously.

_____ 7. Tell me the answer right.

_____ 8. I like to visit my friends, to go to the movies, and swimming.

_____ 9. I want to go home, I need to take medicine.

_____ 10. I need some ingredient for making a good cake.

***

_____ 11. When I am younger, I was healthier.

_____ 12. Even though he did.

_____ 13. She will to learn English one day.

_____ 14. Vietnam has two season.

_____ 15. Although he has an education.

_____ 16. He goes to school every day, he gets a good grade.

_____ 17. He needs to improve his grade and doing his homework.

_____ 18. The books are by the student carried.

_____ 19. They like to discovery new things.

_____ 20. The African students are tallest than the French students.

***

_____ 21. He is a oldest man in class.

_____ 22. Since he was sick he stayed at home.

_____ 23. I went to japan on Saturday.

_____ 24. I met some forign students at GSU.

_____ 25. The man who got in the car wearing white shoes.

_____ 26. I often stay up late doing my homeworks.

_____ 27. All of all I had a good time at the wedding.

_____ 28. The cat and dog sits together because they has been raised to.

_____ 29. When will you be leaving for Chicago

_____ 30. I wonder what does she at work every day.

How to Use an Error Correction Sheet

An Error Correction Sheet is a tool for finding a pattern or patterns of grammatical errors in your essays. It is a way for you and your instructor to analyze and to categorize the kinds of mistakes you are making in your paper in order for you to reduce the errors. This exercise generally reveals a particular pattern, such as verb form errors or article errors, and this will encourage you to study and to learn the grammar that you do not know.

Below are two body paragraphs from a student composition. Here, the instructor has underlined **only** the grammar errors of the paper and numbered the errors. On the adjoining page, you will find the Error Correction Sheet completed for that essay and an analysis at the bottom.

Topic: *Is college a good place to find out who you really are?*

The first year you are in college you <u>taught</u>[1] all of the basic skills that you need. You may learn math, computer science, and sociology, and many more. For all these basic <u>skill</u>[2], you choose which one of those <u>field</u>[3] that fits <u>to</u>[4] you. After you choose your major, you start <u>learn</u>[5] the field that you choose <u>deepler.</u>[6]

<u>On</u>[7] the second year in college, you begin to realize that the major that you choose[8] (MISSING VERB) a fit for you. <u>Eventhough</u>[9] you think that the major you choose is not good for you, you can still change the major that you think is <u>better</u>[10] for you. If you still <u>can not decided</u>[11] what field you are good[12] you can go to the Access Center at the college to get help <u>for choosing</u>[13] your major. You can complete some tests to find out your <u>ability.</u>[14] The results of the test will show what you can do, and the counselors will suggest some fields they think <u>is work</u>[15] best for you, but the choice is yours to decide.

– Nino Radesento

Error Correction Sheet

Use this Error Correction Sheet with one of your essays that has been marked by your teacher. After you finish, analyze the patterns of errors that you make and study the particular grammar area where you made mistakes.

Error (copy your error)	Kind of error (categorize it)	Correction (correct it)	Careless error or new (check)
1. TAUGHT	VERB	ARE TAUGHT	NEW INFORMATION
2. skill	NUMBER	skills	CARELESS
3. FiElD	NUMBER	FiElDS	CARELESS
4. FiTS TO YOU	PREPOSITION	FiTS YOU	NEW
5. lEARN	VERB FORM	lEARNING	CARELESS
6. DEEPLER	W. CHOICE	IN A DEEPER WAY	CARELESS
7. ON	PREPOSITION	IN	CARELESS
8. —	MISSING VERB	BECOMES	NEW
9. EVENTHOUGH	W. CHOICE	IF	CARELESS
10. BETTER	W. CHOICE	BEST	CARELESS
11. CAN NOT DECiDED	VERB FORM	CAN NOT DECiDE	CARELESS
12. —	PREPOSITION	GOOD AT	NEW
13. FOR CHOOSING	PREPOSITION	IN CHOOSING	NEW
14. ABiliTY	NUMBER	ABiliTES	CARELESS
15. is WORk	VERB FORM	WORk	CARELESS

Be sure to write down your errors in order as they appear in your paper. That is the only way the teacher can check them. If you do not understand what kind of error it is, ask! A circle indicates that you left out a word, usually an article or preposition.

Totals: Careless __10__
       New __5__

Kinds of Errors and Number of Errors
1. VERB   5
2. PREPOSITION   4
3. NUMER   3
4. W. CHOICE   3

Error Correction Sheet

Use this Error Correction Sheet with one of your essays that has been marked by your teacher. After you finish, analyze the patterns of errors that you make and study the particular grammar area where you made mistakes.

Error	Kind of error	Correction	Careless error or new
(copy your error)	(categorize it)	(correct it)	(check)

1. _____

2. _____

3. _____

4. _____

5. _____

6. _____

7. _____

8. _____

9. _____

10. _____

11. _____

12. _____

13. _____

Be sure to write down your errors in order as they appear in your paper. That is the only way the teacher can check them. If you do not understand what kind of error it is, ask! A circle indicates that you left out a word, usually an article or preposition.

Totals: Careless _____   **Kinds of Errors and Number of Errors**
        New _____   1. _____   _____
                                   2. _____   _____
                                   3. _____   _____
                                   4. _____   _____

In-Class Compositions – Record Sheet of Errors

Instructions: Put the number by each error you have made after you have completed your error sheet. This record sheet gives you an overview of errors in your essays.

	In-class #1	In-class #2	In-class #3	In-class #4
Sentence Boundaries				
comma splice				
run on				
fragment				
Verb Errors				
verb form				
verb tense				
gerund/infinitive				
Agreement/Number				
agreement				
number				
Serious Errors				
word choice				
word order				
word form				
article				
Minor Errors				
spelling				
punctuation				
capitalization				
Other Errors				
non-English				
Total Error Count				

Grammar Editing Strategies (15 to 20 minutes)

This is an editing guide for your writing. Try to edit for one grammar area at a time, not all at once. A good editing job takes about 5 minutes at each level.

The First Level: Sentence Boundaries

During the first reading of your paper, you should check that all your sentences begin with capital letters and end with periods. Does each sentence have a subject and verb? Does anything look "incomplete" (a fragment)? Do you have commas between independent clauses? One trick in doing this is to read your paper from back-to-front, one sentence at a time. That way an exceptionally long sentence or a short "because" clause will stand out when it is not read in context.

The Second Level: Verb Tense and Verb Form

Since verbs are of critical importance to meaning in a composition, you must spend editing time checking both the time frame and the form. While you are lightly underlining your verbs, ask yourself these questions: What time frame am I writing in? Am I using this time frame consistently? Are my verb forms correct? Have I remembered to use "s" or "es" with third person singular verbs in the present tense?

The Third Level: Nouns, Articles, Number and Agreement (SV)

During the third reading, pay attention to the just nouns and all the determiners that surround the nouns. Look at an individual noun and ask yourself: Is this common noun a count or non-count noun? If there is no other determiner present, what article do I need? Do my determiners or adjectives "match" in number with my nouns? It is also a good time to look at the verbs again to check subject-verb agreement. In this reading, look out for a missing "s" on plural nouns.

The Fourth Level: Word Choice, Word Form, Spelling

Though you may look up individual words as you are writing, now is time to check and re-check any words which you feel might be wrong. The rule of thumb is not to gamble that you are right with any word – check and re-check, especially with a high frequency item in your composition. If a particular phrase does not seem quite right (or is awkward even to you), then reword it to something simpler, something that you know is correct.

The Fifth Level: Your Own Particular Weakness

One last reading is to edit for your own particular weakness that may not be covered in the above four readings. This might be, for example, prepositions or comma use.

Section Three:
Grammar Explanations and Exercises

Sentence Structure
Verbs
Subject-Verb Agreement and Number
Articles
Prepositions
Gerunds and Infinitives
Transformational Exercises

How many mistakes can you find in this advertisement?

Photo by Barbara Hall, London Bridge, Virginia

26

Sentence structure:

In ESL, passing the exit writing exam is very important for all international students who will be taking English courses in college. In order to pass the exam, we must learn to make fewer grammar errors in an essay, and we have to learn to express our ideas in a correct way. For me, as one of the international students in DeKalb College who has finished ESL this quarter, I have learned to correct many of my own errors. One of the most common grammar errors I make is the fragment error. A fragment means an uncompleted sentence without a verb or a subject and sometimes an idea that can not stand by itself.

I have learned to fix the error by underlining the subject once and underlining the verb twice, and then I carefully check whether the sentence is simple, compound, or complex. If the sentence is compound or complex, I know I will have two clauses. Each clause must have at least a subject and a verb. After I learned to correct this error, I know I will never make this error again.

                                                                            –Ying Ye

Sentence Types and Analysis

Many students can write correctly without knowing anything about sentence types and analyzing sentence structure. However, if you have trouble knowing when to stop a sentence or receive "sentence structure" marks on your paper, study the following simple explanation of the four basic sentence types in the English language.

After you have finished, complete the exercises. Finally you are ready analyze sentences using your own writing. Remember when you analyze sentences, you just look for the foundations of the sentence – the subjects, verbs and connectors. You have to ignore many other words in the sentence including adverbs, adjectives, and prepositional phrases. The process is much like looking at the structure of a house and ignoring everything else. Follow these steps:

1. Highlight or put parentheses around the prepositional phrases.
2. Underline your subjects and verbs.
3. Look for any connectors and dependent clauses.
4. Decide whether each sentence is simple, compound, complex, or compound-complex.
5. Look at your sentences to see if you have a variety of sentence types.

Sentence Types

1. SIMPLE SENTENCE

You can use this symbol for a simple sentence.

A simple sentence has one subject and one verb except when it has two subjects or two verbs joined by a conjunction.

The formula for a simple sentence is S + V +(O).
O = object and is optional.

Example: *I go home.*
Example with prepositional phrases: *I go home on Friday after 2 p.m. in my car.*

Simple sentence with a compound subject:
Example: *My sister and I go home together every afternoon.* Subjects: *My sister and I*

Simple sentence with a compound verb:
Example: *My sister goes home and eats dinner quickly.* Verbs: *goes and eats*

28

2. COMPOUND SENTENCE

You can use this symbol
for a compound sentence.

A compound sentence has two independent clauses and some kind of connector between them. It is usually a sentence that is packed with meaning because it has two independent clauses where either one could be separated and stand on its own as a sentence.

The formula for a compound sentence is S + V + connector + S + V.

There are three basic ways to connect independent clauses.

1. Coordinating conjunctions

FANBOYS (for, and, nor, but, or, yet, so) is a mnemonic device that is used to remember the coordinating conjunctions. You must use a comma in front of the coordinating conjunction.

Example: *I am in school now, but I will be working soon.*

2. Transitional expressions (often called **fancy connectors**)
include meanwhile, however, therefore, thus, moreover, etc.

Fancy connectors are surrounded by punctuation: a semi-colon in front and a comma after. They look fancy! This is a good way to remember them and the punctuation which surrounds them.

Example: *I am in school now; however, I will be working soon.*

3. Semi-colons

The semi-colon is not used frequently. It is saved for the special case where the second clause adds to or explains the meaning of the first clause. ESL students tend to overuse the semi-colon. Look at the writing in your academic setting to see how other writers use semi-colons.

Example: *I am in school now; I will be working soon.*

3. COMPLEX SENTENCE

You can use this symbol for a complex sentence.

A complex sentence has one independent clause and one or more dependent clauses. The dependent clause is introduced by a subordinating conjunction such as when, where, that, if, or how. There are many subordinating conjunctions.

The formula for a complex sentence is S + V + (subordinating conjunction) + S + V
(independent clause) + (dependent clause)

Example: *I go home when I finish my work.*

Put a comma after the dependent clause when it precedes the independent clause.

Example: *When I finish my work, I go home.*

Dependent clauses include relative clauses which follow and add information to nouns. This is a complex sentence where the relative pronoun becomes the subject of the dependent clause.

Example: *I saw my sister, who lives in New York, last year.*

Example: *The man who got on the bus was wearing red socks for the holidays.*

4. COMPOUND-COMPLEX SENTENCE

You can use this symbol for a compound-complex sentence.

This sentence is a combination of a compound sentence with one or more dependent clauses.

S + V + (connector) + S + V + subordinating conjunction + S + V
     <u>compound</u>   **<u>complex</u>**

Example: *When I go home, I will cook dinner, and my family will eat it.*

Example: *The students wanted to buy their books at the beginning of the quarter, but the bookstore was very crowded which made the lines move slow.*

Exercise 8: *Analyze the following sentences by putting a single line under the subject and a double line under the verb. Then decide what kind of sentence it is. Put one of the symbols on the line beside the sentence.* for simple, for compound, for complex, and for compound-complex.

1. _____ I am searching for a self-teaching program that will help students learn Windows on the computer.

2. _____ On Wednesday, I will go over to the computer lab, and I will ask them about a program.

3. _____ I hope that they will tell me something positive.

4. _____ If I can't find such a program, I will have to create an exercise for students who do not know how to use Windows on the computer.

5. _____ Students need to know how to save, delete, add, and exit from the computer.

6. _____ This is just the beginning; however, there is much more which students must learn.

7. _____ Unfortunately, there is a steep learning curve for students who are just learning to use the computer.

8. _____ If you are just learning how to use the computer, you can go to the computer lab for help.

9. _____ Many colleges now require that students buy their own computers, so students can use the computers at home.

10. _____ I think this is a good idea because computers will be used in almost all professions that students are majoring in.

11. _____ Do you have a computer at home?

Exercise 9: *Practice writing different types of sentences. Underline your subjects and verbs in each sentence.*

1. Write five simple sentences.
2. Write five compound sentences.
3. Write five complex sentences
4. Write five compound-complex sentences.

Analyzing Sentences and Recognizing Prepositional Phrases

Exercise 10: *Underline the subject(s) in each sentence once and the verb(s) twice. As you underline the subjects and the verbs, analyze each sentence. Write the type of sentence below (simple, compound, complex, or compound-complex). After you have finished, put parenthesis around each prepositional phrase.*

A Simplified Explanation of Global Warming

(1) Many people are talking about the possibility of global warming. (2) Burning fossil fuels, including gas, oil, and coal, releases carbon dioxide which collects in the atmosphere. (3) Carbon dioxide is one of the greenhouse gases. (4) Greenhouse gases act like glass in a greenhouse, and they don't allow heat to escape into space. (5) The increase of heat threatens to bring great changes in climate, and the polar ice caps may melt which will cause seas to rise and coastal cities to flood. (6) The heated earth will change the climate. (7) Temperate zones may become subtropical, so diseases like malaria will move north and south away from the equator. (8) Weather patterns will change in a violent manner as heat is added to the earth. (9) Crops and crop types will be altered. (10) For example, the oak-pine forests of the southeastern United States may be replaced by savannahs and grassland. (11) Scientists predict that the earth's temperature will rise from 1 to 3 1/2 degrees C. (12) Many scientists think the use of fossil fuels must be halted or reduced. (13) If this happens, how will you get to school?

1.	5.	9.	13.
2.	6.	10.	
3.	7.	11.	
4.	8.	12.	

(18 prepositional phrases)

A Look at Sentence Variety in Your Essays:
What Are You Writing at the Sentence Level?

Exercise 11: This is an exercise where you analyze one of your essays for the type of sentence variety that you are using. The point of this analysis is two-fold: to make sure that your writing complexity is sufficient and sophisticated enough for college level work and to make sure that you do not overuse one particular pattern. Choose your most recent essay and refer to the page on "Sentence Types and Analysis" for help. Fill in the analysis.

1. The number of paragraphs in your essay _____.

2. The number of sentences in each paragraph:
   Introduction _____
   Body Paragraph 1 _____
   Body Paragraph 2 _____
   Body Paragraph 3 _____
   Body Paragraph 4 _____
   Conclusion _____

3. Choose the body paragraph that is the longest (i.e., the most developed).
   The number of sentences in this paragraph _____
   A. The number of words in the longest sentence _____
   B. The number of words in the shortest sentence _____

4. Sentence Type Analysis (based on the longest body paragraph):

   A. The number of **simple sentences** in this paragraph _____
      Example: _____
      _____

   B. The number of **compound sentences** in this paragraph _____
      Example: _____
      _____

   C. The number of **complex sentences** in this paragraph _____
      Example: _____ _____
      _____

   D. The number of **compound-complex** sentences in this paragraph _____
      Example: _____
      _____

5. Based on the results of the above, does your essay display sufficient sentence variety?

6. How might you improve your sentence variety and complexity in your next essay?

Sentence Structure Errors

The errors that you make in sentence structure are considered the most serious errors. Below is a short explanation of the three major types of sentence errors.

1. **Fragment: missing either a S or a V, or the idea is incomplete.**

   Incorrect: The car that was sold for $500 and had over 140,000 miles on the engine.
   Correct: The car that was sold for $500 and had over 140,000 miles on the first engine was a lemon.

2. **Comma Splice: two independent clauses joined by a comma.**

   Incorrect: She won the lottery, she promptly spent it.
   Correct: She won the lottery, so she promptly spent it.

3. **Run-on: two independent clauses joined without the correct punctuation or coordinating conjunction.**

   Incorrect: I went to Georgia State for my class I was late.
   Correct: I went to Georgia State for my class, but I was late.

Exercise 12: *Identify the type of sentence error: Frag, CS, or R-O. One of the sentences is correct. Correct all the other sentences.*

_____1. The weather in Georgia now is almost perfect there is little humidity and the temperature drops down at night.

_____2. This is a change from the hot, humid summer weather that comes from the southeast.

_____3. Soon the leaves will turn brown and just drop on the ground the weather in Georgia does not produce stunningly colorful leaves like the northeast.

_____4. Even in the northeast where the temperature drops to just about freezing and the leaves turn a brilliant orange, red, and yellow.

_____5. Many people go to north Georgia to the country fairs country people present a mixture of mountain culture through demonstrations of crafts and playing music.

_____6. The north Georgia apples are ripe, people often buy boxes of them.

_____7. Although winter is coming, it doesn't get very cold in Atlanta most years you only need to throw a couple of more blankets on your bed.

_____8. Many of the out-of-state tourists who drive to the beginning of the Appalachian trail in North Georgia.

_____9. Hikers who are less experienced travel to state parks they find the wide hiking trails much easier there.

_____10. Horseback riding a common outdoor activity in many of these nature trails.

_____11. Maybe you can find some time in your busy life to do some visiting to these places, certainly you will find an outing like that worth your while.

More About Sentence Structure Errors

There are a couple of other common sentence structure errors. Study them carefully. If you tend to make any of the sentence structure errors, consider how it reflects your lack of knowledge about sentence formation and sentence boundaries.

1. **Sentence Boundaries Exceeded:** As a general rule, you can put no more than two independent ideas in one sentence. Therefore, you can only put one coordinating conjunction, or one fancy connector, or only one semi-colon per sentence. Any more ideas in one sentence exceeds the ability of the reader to read quickly. The message load of the sentence is exceeded.

   Error: I went home, and I began to cook some dinner, but there were no fresh vegetables. (This sentence has too many ideas – 3 independent clauses. Reduce to two independent ideas.*)

   Correction: I went home, and I began to cook some dinner. There were no fresh vegetables.

2. **Mixing up sentence types*:** Using a subordinating conjunction to begin a complex sentence but shifting to a compound sentence pattern. Look at the sentence patterns below.

   S + V+ (coordinator) + S + V = compound sentence
   (subordinating conjunction) + S + V, S+ V = complex sentence

   Error: Even though I thought I was late, and I went home without getting the tickets.

   Correction: Even though I thought I was late, I went home without getting the tickets.

   Error: Because you write many essays, and you will become a better writer. (It is easy to correct this error. Just take out the coordinating conjunction and turn the sentence into a complex sentence!)

   Correction: Because you write many essays, you will become a better writer.

*This error is common among Vietnamese, Chinese, and Iranian students. If you make this error, think about the grammatical structure in your first language that is interfering with English. This might help you.

Verbs:
Verb Form
Verb Tenses
Time Frames and Time Words
Irregular Verbs
The Passive Voice
Causative Verbs

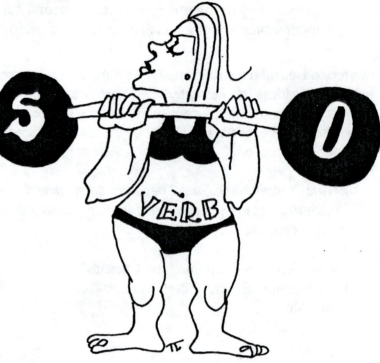

I studied ENSL 017 for ten weeks. In these ten weeks I learned to correct all kinds of errors that I made. However, one of the errors that I learned to correct the most is verb tense. The reason I learned to correct verb tenses a lot was because verb tense was one of the errors that I made all the time. First I learned how to define the time frame in an essay. Then I underlined the verbs. After I underlined the verbs, I decided if the verbs needed to change to be present, past, or future time frame. I think I have improved a lot since I took this class. Only in this class did I learn how to edit by myself, and I think this is a very good skill for students to find their own errors.

– Chanh Ngoc Lam

The error that I frequently made and learned about in this class is the verb tense. Before this class, I used to write paragraphs without considering the time frame. I used to switch from one time frame to another without indicating the time. For example, I used to switch from the present to the past without using the past time indicators like yesterday, last month, or last year. I learned more about tenses and time frames in this class. I learned the twelve tenses. I learned to indicate the new time frame when I changed from one tense to another. In general, I improved a lot in understanding and indicating the verb tenses.

– Robiel T. Teclemichael

Verbs

Correct use of verb tenses and forms is very important in English. Verbs carry much of the main meaning of the sentence, and verb suffixes and auxiliaries indicate the time. Verbs are the powerhouses of our language.

There are two main types of verb errors. Try to distinguish between the two types. *Verb form* is an error where the tense has been incorrectly formed. *Verb tense* is an error where an incorrect tense has been chosen for the meaning. Although the grammar of verbs is very complex in English, every student can easily learn the basic grammar and be able to use verbs correctly. This short section on verbs is designed for students who are still confused about the basic forms and/or uses of verbs.

Verb Forms

One way to begin to learn about verbs is to study and memorize the 12 traditional tenses in English. This includes the perfective and the progressive aspect. The progressive and perfect tenses use auxiliary verbs (be and have) in their formation. The simple tenses are used more often than other tenses and are simple to form. They also do not have auxiliary verbs (be and have). By memorizing the names of the verb tenses and how to form them, you will be able to write with more verb control. Practice them until you can recreate them without looking at the book.

Simple: Future   (*formed with "will"*) I will go home soon.
         Present: John eats vegetable every day. (*add "s" in the third-person singular*)
         Past*:   They walked to the meeting every month.

*Regular past tense verbs are formed by adding "ed." Check the list of irregular past tense verbs at the end of this section.

Progressive: (formed with be + ing)
         Future: Soon the students will be returning.
         Present: She is looking for a good used car for her son.
         Past: The bookstore clerks were ordering the books for the fall quarter.

Perfect: (formed with have + past participle)
         Future: In five days, she will have completed the exercises.
         Present: I have been in Atlanta since 1967.
         Past: The boy had finished his paper route by two o'clock Sunday.

Mixed: (perfect and progressive – formed with have + be [past participle] + ing)
         Future: The aunt will have been visiting Europe for three months.
         Present: I have been reading this book for two hours.
         Past: The girl had been eating her ice cream for only five minutes.

Study the verb forms before you do the exercises. Try to do these sentences without looking at the previous page.

Exercise 13: *Write a sentence for each of the following tenses.*

Simple   A. future

                    B. present

                    C. past

Progressive   *(be + ing)*
                    A. future

                    B. present

                    C. past

Perfect   *(have + past participle)*
                    A. future

                    B. present

                    C. past

Mixed   *(have + be [past participle] + ing)*
                    A. future perfect continuous

                    B. present perfect continuous

                    C. past perfect continuous

Exercise 14: *Underline the verb phrase(s) and identify the tense(s) in each sentence.*

_____ 1. Mr. John was cutting his lawn when Mrs. John called him.

_____ 2. She will be going to Peru to visit the mountains.

_____ 3. After she had gone, he came in looking sheepishly.

_____ 4. Marie has been going to the doctor frequently.

_____ 5. I went to the University of Washington in Seattle before I transferred to GSU.

_____ 6. She is acting up in front of her mother.

_____ 7. I will have been a vegetarian for over five years now.

Exercise 15: *Change the following sentences into the present perfect continuous.*

1. We have a great deal of fun with our new computer recently.

_____

2. I wait for a reply from that business ever since February.

_____

3. It rain steadily since two o'clock this afternoon.

_____

4. Ms. Johnson worked for the company for ten years.

_____

Exercise 16: *State the name(s) of the tense(s).*

1. We ran home after the football game. _____

2. We had been running since we saw the lightning. _____,_____

3. I study all the time. _____

4. When was studying when her mother came home. _____, _____

5. When will you be leaving for Japan? _____

6. Have you seen the latest dollar exchange rate? _____

7. The new foreign students will be coming to college to take the English Placement test soon.

_____

8. Aren't you glad that you've already finished that exam? _____, _____

9. We have had too much trouble with my car. _____

10. Now it is working just fine. _____

11. Did she take a new name after she married? _____

12. Has she changed your major again? _____

13. Are you coming to visit soon? _____

14. Have you seen the new renovation of the bookstore? _____

Verb Tenses

Learning to use the correct tense is more difficult that learning the verb forms. **Writing a sentence:** When you choose a tense for an individual sentence, the time words or the context of the sentence should be enough to tell you which tense to use. **Writing a paragraph:** When you are writing a paragraph, the tenses are organized and related in a cohesive way using the time frame that was chosen at the beginning of the paragraph and the time words that are used in the paragraph. Look at a few of the general guidelines for tense use below. This section is only a quick review of the verb tenses and the most common problems of ESL students. After you have finished this section, study the section on time frames and time words.

Common Verb Tense Problems for ESL Students:

1. DO use the simple present and simple past tenses: Native speakers use the simple tense the most, both in writing and speaking. It is estimated that simple tenses are used about 70-80% of the time in academic writing. These tenses are the easiest to use. The use of the simple tenses does not mean that what you are saying is simple. Listen to the tense choice of native speakers. Look at printed material around you. Notice what kind of tenses are used. When you are in doubt, choose a simple tense.

2. DON'T overuse the progressive: ESL students tend to overuse the continuous tense. This tense is used to express ideas that are happening in the future, now, or in the past. It describes actions and is not generally used with stative verbs. An exception to this rule is the use of progressive in Indian English. Indian English uses the progressive tense almost like American English speakers use the present tense. Overuse of the progressive is an easy mistake to correct if noticed. The solution is to change from the progressive tense to a simple tense. The progressive tense is often used with the time word "while."

> **While** I was doing my homework, the door bell rang.
> My brother was cooking **while** I was cutting up the vegetables.

Exercise 17: *Look at the verbs in each sentence. Change them from the progressive to the simple tenses. Listen to how awkward they "sound" in the progressive tense.*

1. I am feeling bad about the way I performed in the recital.

2. He was considering his future as he signed up for his classes.

3. When will you be seeing the doctor tomorrow?

4. The fire was happening right before end of the last period.

5. I am knowing the people in my neighborhood very well.

6. In the future I will be learning my job and learning about the modern workplace too.

3. WATCH OUT FOR the present perfect vs. the simple past: The present perfect is used to cross over the past/present time barrier and express something that happened in the past but is still continuing in the present. This tense is usually used with the time words "since" and "for." Unlike the present perfect, the past tense is used to describe an action that has ended. Look at the following examples.

> I **have lived** in Atlanta for 25 years. (*implies that I still live here*)
> I **lived** in Atlanta for 25 years. (*implies that I don't live in Atlanta now*)

The present perfect is a tense that is frequently used both in oral and written speech. It is important to understand the difference between the present perfect and past tense.

Exercise 18: *Use the correct form of the verb in parentheses in each sentence. Choose between the past tense and the present perfect tense.*

1. Some time ago, we (hear) some bad news about our friend in China.
2. Susan (travel) to California many times to see the redwood forests in Mendocino County.
3. I (see) that movie three times already.
4. Before her graduation, Chan (apply) to IBM for an internship.
5. Abdoul and Isaac (finish not) their research papers yet.
6. Our neighbors (return) from a Canadian wilderness trip yesterday.
7. From the beginning of the quarter until now, she (turn) in 90% of the lab reports.

4. DON'T OVERUSE the past perfect: The past perfect is used much less frequently than the present perfect in English. It is often written in a complex sentence with time words to help the reader/listener to distinguish the time sequence of the events. It is used to describe an action in the past before another action in the past. The first action (oldest) uses the past perfect. The most recent action uses the simple past.

> The student **had finished** the homework before the paper **needed** to be turned in.
> When the school quarter **had ended,** the students **went** on break.

Exercise 19: *Change the verbs in the following sentences. Use the past perfect to indicate which action happened first.*

1. Before the car (go) off the interstate, the tire (hit) a nail and other rubbish on the road.

2. The weather channel (remind) us that the wind (blown) very hard the week before last.

3. After her husband (burn) the rice twice in one week, the wife (bought) a rice cooker.

4. Before the salesperson (total) her monthly averages, the boss (propose) new bonuses.

5. Joe (admit) that he (help) his brother through the entire math tutoring session.

Time Frames

In a paragraph, verbs are organized in time frames. A time frame is a broad concept of time. Paragraphs are usually written in one of the three time frames: future, present, or past. A paragraph is set up in one time frame. Then the writer stays in the same time frame unless a time word is chosen to shift to another time frame. Look at a typical clustering of tenses and corresponding time words in each time frame.

Future Time Frame	**Present Time Frame**	**Past Time Frame**
Tenses used:	**Tenses used:**	**Tenses used:**
simple future	simple present	simple past
future progressive	present progressive	past progressive
future perfect progressive	present perfect	past perfect
simple present	present perfect progressive	past perfect prog.
Examples of future time words:	present time words:	past time words:
tomorrow	today	yesterday
the next day	presently	last month
in a few minutes	right now	a few years ago
in the future	currently	in 1996
in the year 2001	this afternoon	later today

Time shifting or time traveling: When students are not aware of time frames, they will often shift from the present to the past and back without realizing what tenses are being used. **This is a common problem for students who come from language backgrounds where verbs are not individually marked to indicate time.** The best way to correct this problem is to underline each verb and write the tense above it. Note the time frame of the paragraph and the time words. When students become aware of how tenses must be consistent in the paragraph, the errors usually end.

These exercises become progressively harder as they move from simple identification of verbs tenses to a recognition of incorrect verb tenses and forms. The last exercise is the hardest and demands that you pay strict attention to both time frames and time words within the paragraph.

Exercise 20: *Read the following paragraph and then do two things: Underline the verbs, and write the name of the verb tense above it. All the verbs are correct.*

Since I moved to Atlanta, I have changed in many ways. First of all, when I started teaching at DeKalb College in 1989, I was living in Athens, Georgia, and therefore I was commuting to work each day. The drive back and forth would take up about three hours of my day. I was tired during that first year of teaching at DeKalb. However, in 1990 I actually moved to Atlanta and bought a small house that I rented with a roommate. After I had lived with her for one year, I decided to get married, and my husband moved into my house. One year later, I gave birth to our son, Gabriel. Boy, my life sure has changed in the past five years!

Exercise 21: *Read the following paragraph. Underline the verbs and correct the tenses.*

In 1998 all the public colleges and universities change to the semester system. This change will mean that classes begin in August and end in early May. For two years, teachers been adjusting the curriculum to the semester system. Presently most colleges were on the semester system, so Georgia join most other states. There were some advantages and disadvantages. Students will have to pay more tuition in August, but they only have to pay and register twice. Since all public colleges and universities are change to this system, transferring to another college in Georgia remain the same. Be sure to find out how these changes will affect the classes you take right now and well as the classes you plan to take.

Exercise 22: *Read the following paragraph. Underline the verbs, and correct the verb forms and the verb tenses.*

Five years ago, Jing Mei has been a student at Beijing University where she has gotten a degree in chemistry. When she camed to the United States in 1991, her English were not so good, so she has took classes at an intensive English language school. After she finish the classes, she enroll at Georgia Tech to continued her studies in chemistry. She soon quitted because she does not feel that those classes were prepare her for her major which was engineering. Her life changes a lot in five years.

Exercise 23: *This is a very difficult exercise! Look both at the time frame of the paragraph and the time words in each sentence. Write the correct tense.*

While I (walk) across the campus the other day, I (meet) my old friend John, whom I (see, not) since spring quarter. Naturally, we (stop) to talk to each other for a few minutes. I (ask) him how he (do) in his classes this summer. He (tell) me that he (take) a course in English this quarter. He (say) that he (complete) the ESL courses two quarters before, and by next quarter, he (be) ready to take English 201.

"Until now," he (say), "I (take, always) the 12 credits which (make) a minimum full-time program for a foreign student. However, I (enroll) for 15 credits next quarter. Then I (lose, not) so much time. You see, I (interest) in getting my degree as soon as possible. In the future I (transfer) to a technical school and (graduate) in computer science. "He also (say) that he (ask, already) his advisor for permission to take an extra two credit class.

(See "A Contrastive Look at the Grammar of Six Languages" in the front of this text for information about verb tense differences.)

Irregular Verbs

Many students in advanced writing have still not learned the past tense irregular verbs. This list is provided to review the most common of the past tense irregular verbs. Take a piece of paper and put it over the last two columns, so only the base form is showing. Quickly write the past tense and the past participle for each irregular verb. Work for about 10 minutes. Go back and check your work. Study the verbs that you don't know. Be sure that you can spell all the irregular forms correctly. Continue working through the list until you have checked yourself for all the verbs.

Base form	Past	Past participle	Base form	Past	Past participle
am, is, are	was, were	been	hold	held	held
beat	beat	beaten, beat	hurt	hurt	hurt
become	became	become	keep	kept	kept
begin	began	begun	know	knew	known
bend	bent	bent	leave	left	left
bite	bit	bitten	lose	lost	lost
bleed	bled	bled	make	made	made
blow	blew	blown	meet	met	met
break	broke	broken	pay	paid	paid
bring	brought	brought	read	read	read
build	built	built	ride	rode	ridden
buy	bought	bought	ring	rang	rung
catch	caught	caught	run	ran	run
choose	chose	chosen	say	said	said
come	came	come	see	saw	seen
cut	cut	cut	send	sent	sent
dig	dug	dug	shake	shook	shaken
do	did	done	show	showed	shown
draw	drew	drawn	shut	shut	shut
drink	drank	drunk	sing	sang	sung
drive	drove	driven	sit	sat	sat
eat	ate	eaten	spend	spent	spent
fight	fought	fought	stand	stood	stood
find	found	found	steal	stole	stolen
fly	flew	flown	swim	swam	swum
forget	forgot	forgotten	take	took	taken
freeze	froze	frozen	tell	told	told
get	got	gotten	think	thought	thought
give	gave	given	throw	threw	thrown
go	went	gone	understand	understood	understood
have	had	had	wear	wore	worn
hide	hid	hidden, hid	win	won	won
hit	hit	hit	write	wrote	written

45

The Passive Voice

The passive voice can be added to verbs creating a difference in meaning and a difference in grammatical form from the active voice. In a clause with an active verb, the subject is "responsible" for the action described, as in this example:

> **Faculty members often forget to lock their office doors when they go to computer labs to print something.**

Who did the forgetting? The answer is the faculty members – that is, the subject of the sentence. We know this because the verb is active. But look at the difference in the following sentence where the verb is passive:

> **Janet's purse was stolen from her office last week when she went to the computer room and forgot to lock her office.**

Who did the stealing? Certainly not Janet! She was not responsible for the action; she only suffered the effects! We know this because the verbs are passive.

In order to avoid errors with the passive, a good strategy is to memorize how to form it so that you can do automatically. Always remember to put the verb "to be" in the tense you need and add the past participle to it. Here are some basic passive structures.

Present: am, is, are + past participle
Example: Campus mail **is delivered** by noon to faculty offices.

Present Progressive: am being, is being, are being + past participle
Example: A new wing **is being added** to our office building this year.

Past: was, were + past participle
Example: All final grades **were posted** on the main doors of campus.

Past Progressive: was being, were being + past participle
Example: When I came to register, parking decals **were being handed** out to students.

Future: will be + past participle
Example: The final grades **will be sent** to all students by January 1.

With Modal/Present: modal + be= past participle
Example: Revisions of papers **can be done** quickly with a computer.

With Infinitive: to + be + past participle
Example: Applications are **to be accepted** in person only.

Exercise 24: *Read the following short article from the DeKalb College newspaper, The Collegian. Find the six passive form verbs used and write them in the following blanks.*

Polishing Cloth issues excellence

By **Thomas J. Hadley**
Editor-in-Chief

This years Sixth edition of the *Polishing Cloth* has been awarded third prize in the southern division of Community College Humanities Association magazine contest- in student writing.

The award was given November 1 in New Orleans at the national conference.

The reception was held on October 5 at 6pm on Central campus. the featured speaker was Dr. Neil B. Shulman, Associate Professor at Emory University school of Medicine.

There have been 16 issues of the Polishing Cloth published since 1985. In 1992 production and distribution went to a national level. It is available in all DeKalb bookstores.

It is designed to provide accessible models in the writing class room - students can see how their peers have successfully completed assignments.

It can be used by instructors in English, Developmental Studies and English as a Second Language. It receives no funds other than the price paid by students buying the book, which last year exceeded $16.

This year the editors, Kendall / Hunt, and Follet College Stores (who manage the college bookstores) have cooperated to reduce the price to $11.

They hope a more affordable price will encourage more instructors to adopt the text for their classes and more students to buy the book for the model papers which reflect most college writing assignments.

The Polishing Cloth is recognized nationally.

At the inauguration of DeKalb College President Jacquelyn M. Belcher in May, 1996, Dr. David R. Pierce, President of the American Association of Community Colleges, commented that the college community "looks forward to each new edition of *The Polishing Cloth,* which has gained national recognition for its creative use of exemplary student composition to encourage better student writing in the class room."

1. _____ from (paragraph ___) is the passive form of _____ tense.

2. _____ from (paragraph ___) is the passive form of _____ tense.

3. _____ from (paragraph ___) is the passive form of _____ tense.

4. _____ from (paragraph ___) is the passive form of _____ tense.

5. _____ from (paragraph ___) is the passive form of _____ tense.

6. _____ from (paragraph ___) is the passive form of _____ tense.

(Note: The passive voice can only be used with transitive verbs, that is, verbs with direct objects. Look at the Preposition Section – Extra Prepositions for a further discussion of transitive and intransitive verbs.)

Using the Passive Voice

The active voice is preferred in most academic writing because it is more immediate, alive and direct than the passive voice. However the passive voice is deliberately chosen in certain situations including when the action is emphasized, when the writer doesn't know who the subject is, and when the writer doesn't want to reveal who the subject is. Often the passive voice is used in scientific writing, in giving instructions, and describing the decisions of organizations. Look at the following examples and notice that it would be difficult to use the active voice.

Examples: The monkeys were examined for the herpes virus.
              The students were registered after a long day of waiting.
              The college policy was reevaluated and changed for the new semester system.

Exercise 25: *Below is a copy of some instructions for parents of boys in the Atlanta Boys Choir. Read the passage and identify the passive verbs by underlining them. (You should find thirteen.) Be careful to underline all parts of each verb: the first auxiliary, any additional form of BE that may be used, and the past participle form of the verb itself. Then discuss with classmates why the passive is used in each case and how the active voice would sound if used.*

The Atlanta Boy Choir, Inc.
1215 Ponce de Leon Avenue
Atlanta, Georgia 30306

MOST IMPORTANT INFORMATION

<u>Ticket Monies and Tuition</u> - All ticket monies and tuition must be paid on Wednesday, December 3. If tuition is not paid on time, there will be a $15.00 late fee that will be charged. <u>Choir Robes</u> will be distributed to the boys the week before the concerts with instructions.

December 12 and 13 Concerts at St. Luke's Church

1. St. Luke's Church is located approximately four blocks south of the Fox Theater and is a dark, red brick church.
2. Boys are to be deposited at 6:00 P.M. at the front entrance.
3. Although boys are deposited at 6:00 P.M., parents are not permitted in the church until the doors open at 7:30 P.M.
4. Cameras and recording equipment of any kind are strictly forbidden at all Boy Choir concerts.
5. Boys are retrieved in the Church Hall at the end of the concert at about 9:30 P.M. No boy will be released early, and no one except boys and official counselors are permitted backstage.

Thank you for your patience and cooperation. Once again, all these things are done to help insure the safety of the boys and to provide a professional atmosphere for their performing.

Causative Verbs
A Note about a Special Group of Verbs

Commonly called **causative verbs** in many ESL grammar books, this small, though regularly used group of verbs, does **CAUSE** trouble because they break some general rules we know about verb forms.

Have you heard people say things like this before?

> Why don't you ever let me do the things I like?
> My mother always makes me take out the trash on Sunday.
> My sister has never helped me finish my chores!
> I can't do that. Why don't you have Trang pick up that heavy box for you?

Four verbs LET, MAKE, HELP, HAVE – use this special grammatical structure:

Subject	+ Causative Verb (in any tense)	+ Object	+ Base Form of 2nd Verb	+ Rest of Sentence

Grammarian Roland Caissie suggests that CAUSATIVE VERBS are similiar to a puppeteer that carefully controls the movements of the puppet.

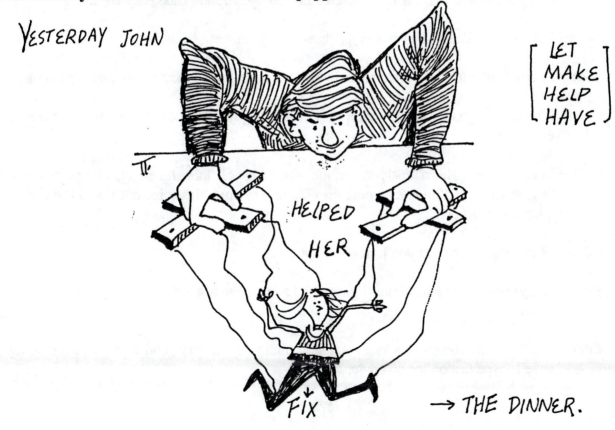

Exercise 26: *Edit the following sentences for errors in causative verbs.*

1. It was a good experience to make me adapted quickly to life in the United States.

2. Finding a good job that lets you be respected by others and enjoys life is very important.

3. Nothing else could help my uncle to stay alive, and finally he was relieved to be back at his home.

4. When Addis saw me, he made me promised to take care of myself and to be a good student in college.

5. Uncle Zack encouraged me to let him to take me to the park.

6. The trees and plants in Atlanta are beautiful, and they help the environment balancing.

7. These features make Atlanta seems like a city in the forest.

Exercise 27: *Correct the errors in the conversation, paying attention to causative verbs.*

Eden: Does your writing instructor make you writing a lot of essays in class?

Safi: I'll say she does. She has us completed one composition in class each week.

Eden: Does she usually make you to type them if they are out of class?

Safi: We don't have to, but I often have my brother typing my papers when they are lengthy.

Eden: That sounds great! Your brother must be a nice guy. What does he make you to do in exchange?

Safi: Good question. He routinely makes me washed his car though last night he made me took the garbage out. I'd prefer typing than doing those insulting jobs, but I'm just too slow at typing right now.

Eden: Why hasn't he helped you learning to type?

Safi: He says he doesn't have time. I guess I'll have to take a word processing class next quarter.

Eden: Since you are computer science major, I think this is a very good idea. You are going to have to type fast on the computer.

Subject-Verb Agreement and Number:

Subject-Verb Agreement Rules
Editing for Subject-verb Agreement
Number Errors
Editing for Number Errors
Identifying the Rules
More Practice

Subject-Verb Agreement

Basic Rule:. A third person singular subject needs to "agree" with any verb in the present tense. An "s" (ies, es) is added to the end of the verb.

Example: Mary drives to school along I-85. (Mary is a third person singular subject.)

Look at the two auxiliary verbs and their forms:

	to be		to have	
	singular	*plural*	*singular*	*plural*
First person	I am	we are	I have	we have
Second person	you are	you are	you have	you have
Third person	he, she, it is	they are	he, she, it has	they have

Rule 1: Intervening phrases. Sometimes the subject is separated from the verb by a phrase or clause. This does not influence the relationship between the subject and the verb.
Example: A student who comes to all classes is responsible.

Rule 2: Compound subjects. A compound subject is considered plural and has no "s."
Example: French and art history are my favorite subjects.

Rule 3: Here/There. In sentences with "here" and "there" the subject follows the verb.
Examples: There are many students who need extra help.
Here is the one book that I promised you.

Rule 4: Indefinite pronouns. Singular indefinite pronouns take a singular verb. These include any, anybody, anyone, anything, each, either, everybody, everyone, everything, neither, nobody, no one, nothing, somebody, someone, something.
Example: Everyone has to bring the English/English dictionary to class.

Rule 5: Gerunds and infinitives. If the subject of the sentence is a gerund or infinitive, the verb is singular. If there are two gerunds or infinitives, the subject is plural.
Examples: Studying at the library is what I do every night.
Studying and working are the two activities of most college students.

Rule 6: Amounts. Where the subject is an amount, distance, or time, it is considered singular.
Examples: Six dollars is not much mone to spend in our times.
Three thousand miles is about the distance from here to California.
Four hours is a long time to take an exam!

Editing for Subject - Verb Agreement

Editing for subject-verb agreement errors is easy. Underline the subject in every sentence and clause and draw a line to the verb it belongs to. Check to see if the subject is in the third person singular and the verb has an "s."

Exercise 28: *The first sentence is done for you. Finish the paragraph by underlining the subject and drawing an arrow to the verb. Correct the errors that you find. After you finish these exercises, follow the same process using your own writing.*

If you want to join cyberspace, you can get an e-mail address and begin to communicate through the internet! At DeKalb College every registered student can get an e-mail address and password. This allow the student to have a mail box to receive mail and also allow the student to send mail to anyone, anywhere in the world who have an e-mail address. Many teachers is using e-mail to send out assignments and comment on students' papers.

When students first learn how to use e-mail, they will probably feel like they does when they learns anything – a little stupid and confused. However, everyone have to learn sometime, and generally teachers and computer assistants is polite and understanding with new learners. Soon after you learn to use e-mail, you will be writing to your friends, writing to your family, and doing class work on the internet. Welcome to cyberspace!

***

The consumption of paper continue to rise all over the world. Currently the world consume five times as much paper as it did in 1950 and by the year 2010 the usage will double. Usage in industrial countries are 10 times greater than in developing countries. The market for pulp and paper is growing, and this are the major driving force behind the development of the single type of tree plantation. This type of plantation are called monoculture. These monoculture plantations often replaces natural forests. It take 75,000 trees alone to print the Sunday run of the *New York Times*. (Adapted from *Vital Signs, 1997*, World Watch Institute.)

Number Errors

Basic Rule: To make nouns plural, add "s" ("ies," "es"). This applies to count nouns only. Number errors are much harder than agreement to catch in your work. Many languages do not use "s" to indicate that a noun is plural. Also in oral speech, the "s" is at the end of words and is often not heard.

Example: I saw many items for sale at the book store.

Rule 1: Noncount nouns do not add "s" and are considered singular. This includes words like homework, information, software, clothing, jewelry and furniture. If you are unsure whether a noun is count or noncount, look it up in an ESL dictionary. Many nouns can be both count and noncount. You must be sure which meaning you are using.

Example: The teacher assigned three pages of homework in the text.

Rule 2: Demonstrative adjectives must agree with the noun. For example, *this* and *that* are singular and *these* and *those* are plural. If your noun is plural, you must use *these* or *those*. If your noun is singular, you must use *this* or *that*.

Example: These computers were on sale, but they did not have enough memory.

Rule 3: When one item is singled out from a group (plural noun), the plural noun must have "s." This often occurs with the phrase "one of _____."

Example: One of the students in my class is taking 20 hours.

Rule 4: Adjectives may be mistaken for nouns and made plural.

Incorrect: She was a sixteen years-old student in college. (The noun is "student.")
Correct: She was a sixteen year-old student in college.
Correct: She was sixteen years old. (In this case the noun is "years" and is plural.)

Rule 5: Pronoun use must be consistent. If you use the singular pronoun "he" or "she," don't switch to the plural pronoun "they."

Incorrect: She went to see their sister in Kentucky.
Correct: She went to see her sister in Kentucky.

Incorrect: Everyone needs to use their ESL dictionary for the exit writing.
Correct : Everyone needs to use his or her ESL dictionary for the exit writing.

Editing for Number Errors

Editing for number errors is much more difficult that editing for subject-verb agreement errors, but editing techniques will help you become aware of whether you need an "s" or not.

Exercise 29: *Underline each noun in the paragraph. Then ask yourself if the noun is plural or singular. Check on the preceding page to review the rules if you get confused. The first sentence is completed for you. After you have finished this exercise, underline all the nouns in your work and check for number errors.*

Urban <u>forestry</u> is becoming a field that many urban and suburban <u>residents</u> are interested in. There is more interest in urban forestry as people feel the need to make city more livable by increasing the green spaces as well as by preserving the green spaces that exist. This interest is primarily centered on tree but includes all kind of vegetation. *(3 errors)*

This fall a conference on Urban Forestry with the theme "Cities by Nature's Design" will be held in downtown Atlanta. It will attract environmentalist, city planner, and urban foresters. People will gather from all across the United State to meet and discuss how to integrate natural resource in urban area. *(5 errors)*

Individuals who are interested in "greening the city" can do his part by planting a tree in his yard, helping other group in tree planting, and by donating money to organization such as Trees Atlanta and Park Pride who plant tree full-time. There is another area that ordinary citizens can participate in. People who are concerned about preserving green space can stay active in effort to write laws protecting historic tree and work on other tree ordinances that seek to regulate cutting down tree. *(9 errors)*

The city of Atlanta has one of the strongest tree ordinance that exists in the nation. This grew out of a grass-roots effort to protect tree and preserve the canopy in the city. This three-years old ordinance is currently being enforced by the City Arborist with the help of people who live in the neighborhood. Because of the continuing effort of Atlantan to protect and preserve tree, Atlanta is often called "a city in a forest." *(6 errors)*

Agreement and Number Errors: Identifying the Rules

Exercise 30: *Write one sentence that has an agreement error and one sentence that has a number error. Write the number of the rule that is broken.*

Agreement:_____

_____Rule:_____

Number:_____

_____Rule:_____

Exercise 31: *Identifying sentence-level agreement and number errors. Correct the errors in each sentence.*

1. Besides that, he loves music and enjoys fixing thing like car or old piece of furniture.

2. He takes a special interest in baseball as every American do.

3. Traveling have also been one of his hobby.

4. In his free time, he like to spend time with his pets which includes a dog and two cat.

5. She always have made good grade in school.

6. These cloth are much too small for me.

7. Juanita's first job was at the Dairy Queen where she worked for seven month.

8. I only had a few friend when I moved here.

9. I saw a few peoples at the movie.

10. All of this items, whether in the bathroom or in the kitchen, is meant to help us.

11. Calculus always give me a headache.

12. I hate going places that don't have a beach.

13. My father always makes me do some homeworks before I go out at night.

14. My cousin, who is fifteen year old, works at a grocery store.

15. Swimming laps are an exercise that I do in the winter.

16. Juan and Donald is swimming instructors during the summer.

17. The tourists who got on the bus is going to tour the Jimmy Carter Library.

18. Someone have taken all the white chalk from the classroom.

19. The washing machine which has a cycle of twenty-five minutes are broken.

Just How Serious Are Agreement and Number Errors?
More Practice

Exercise 32: *In the following student essay, the student had many problems with the third person singular verb in the present tense. Read over the essay and pay attention to verbs. Correct the s-v agreement errors. There are also some number errors.*

Every country in the world have different holiday of its own. In my country, Vietnam, the holiday called "Tet" is most important and special to everyone. During two week of those holiday, members of my family comes back home to remember our ancestors who passed away, to meet and enjoy the holiday together. It is the time that people has the chance to appreciate and to get together to express their feeling.

The week before the New Year come, my family and I starts to do something to make our house clean and to have plenty of food. I usually cleans up around my house to make it looks different. My sister, Thao, take care of food and go to the market to buy items in order to refill them. Decorating our rooms are my brother's duty. He always replace the new calendar every year and sometimes put some new photographs or pictures in the living room. He love flowers, so he buy a lot of fresh flowers and try to put them in a vase. I clean up the place where we puts incense to remember our ancestors. Everything seem fresh and new, so we thinks we remember our ancestors with respect.

In short, the Vietnamese New Year or "Tet" is very meaningful to me. At this time of the year, my friends comes to my house and we plays card or bingo and enjoys delicious food. My family who live in different places get back together after a year of being apart.

– Phuong Trinh

Articles:

Types of Nouns
Kinds of Determiners
The Article Chart
Two Article Rules
The Concept of Definite and Indefinite
Exercises

Writing is the hardest thing I have learned in English. I make many mistakes when I write an essay in English.

One of my serious errors is using articles correctly. In my language, Korean, we don't have any articles such as English has. I always forget to use articles or use them incorrectly.

Fortunately I am getting better writing in English after I learned how I can correct my errors. I learned to underline every noun and define what kind of noun it is. This makes it easy to find and stop my errors. I still make mistakes in my writing, but I am trying to write as correctly as I can.

– Ji-Su Song

I have learned more in this class than I expected. First of all, I had big problems with articles. At the beginning of the class I usually missed putting them in the right place. On the other hand, I would put them before noncount or plural nouns. Although I tried hard to correct my biggest mistake, I needed some time "to come to the point." I correct this mistake by reading newspapers and underlining all the articles I would see. Not using articles caused a lot of frustration for me because people would try to correct me. The corrections were so often and in ever sentence I would say.

– Minya B.

Articles

Many linguists consider using articles correctly as one of the last stages of learning English. At an advanced level, ESL students are expected to control the article rules with about 90% mastery before going into college-level English classes. If you are having trouble understanding when and what kind of article to use, read through the first two sections below to understand the grammar vocabulary necessary to choose the correct article. Then study the article chart and memorize the article rules. Finally, consider the concepts of what makes a noun *definite* or *indefinite*. The exercises at the end will give you some practice applying the explanations. The test of understanding the article system is to apply these rules and concepts to your own writing.

> **What you need to know to master article use:**
> 1. **Types of nouns: count/non-count and singular/plural**
> 2. **The definition and kinds of determiners**
> 3. **The article chart and/or the two article rules**
> 4. **The concept of definite/indefinite**

1. Types of Nouns

Count nouns (such as *book, table, pen*) can be counted and made plural (*books, tables, pens*). Some count nouns (such as *person, child, goose*) have irregular plurals (*people, children, geese*).

Non-count nouns are nouns that cannot be counted and do not have plural forms (*like air, information, homework*). Non-count nouns are treated as singular nouns.

Some nouns can be either count or non-count depending on their meaning in a particular sentence.
> Examples: *I have had three conversations with my teacher.* **(count)**
> *Extended conversation is one method to learn English.* **(non-count)**

Exercise 39: *Classify each noun according to whether it is count or noncount. Some nouns are both. If you are unsure, look up the noun in an ESL dictionary.*

Nouns	Count	Non-count	Both
1. homework	_____	_____	_____
2. equipment	_____	_____	_____
3. keyboard	_____	_____	_____
4. software	_____	_____	_____
5. water	_____	_____	_____

2. Kinds of Determiners

Articles belong to a system of determiners. Determiners include demonstrative adjectives *(this, that, these, those);* quantifiers *(some, any, every, one, two);* and possessive determiners *(my, your, our, her).* If a singular count noun has a determiner, an article is not needed.

Exercise 40: *Identify the determiners by underlining them. Notice that when a noun is preceded by a determiner, there is no indefinite article (a or an).*

Many people go to college without any idea of what they want to major in or what courses they want to take. Every student has questions about the courses when he/she first registers. If a student does not go through orientation, the first chance a student has to ask some questions is during registration. Unfortunately, this is not a relaxing time to ask questions because everybody is trying to register as fast as possible. However, the Access Center is open all quarter, and students can walk in and get information about their courses and other information.

3. The Article Chart

The following chart summarizes the article system. This chart can be used like a computer flow chart by students to decide if an article is needed and which one to choose.

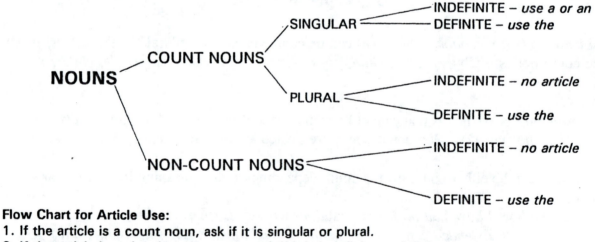

Flow Chart for Article Use:
1. If the article is a count noun, ask if it is singular or plural.
2. If the article is a singular count noun, ask if it is indefinite or definite.
3. If the singular count noun is indefinite, use **a** or **an**.
4. If the singular count noun is definite, use **the**.

1. If the article is a plural count noun, ask if it is indefinite or definite.
2. If the article indefinite, use **no article**.
3. If the article is definite, use **the**.

1. If the noun is a non-count noun, ask if it is indefinite or definite.
2. If the noun is indefinite, use **no article**.
3. If the noun is definite, use **the**.

```
┌─────────────────────────────────────────────────────────────────────────┐
│                        Two Article Rules                                  │
│                                                                           │
│          The following rules will help to determine when and what kind    │
│    of article needs to be used.  If you are having trouble with articles, │
│    memorize the rules.                                                     │
│                                                                           │
│    Rule 1:  A singular count noun needs an article or a determiner.        │
│          Choose a or an if the noun is indefinite.  Choose the if the      │
│          noun is definite                                                  │
│                                                                           │
│    Rule 2:  A plural or noncount noun does not need an article unless      │
│          it is definite.                                                   │
│          Choose: the if the noun is definite.  Choose no article (O) if    │
│          the noun is not definite.                                         │
│                                                                           │
└─────────────────────────────────────────────────────────────────────────┘
```

4. The Concept of Definite/Indefinite

A and *an* are indefinite articles that refer to a non-specific or indefinite singular count noun.   *Example: I eat an apple a day*.

The is the definite article. It refers to a specific or definite count or non-count noun.   *Example: I especially like the apples from north Georgia*.

Study the five guidelines which make nouns definite. If a noun is definite, *the* is used instead of *a*, or *an* or no *article*. Notice that in four of the factors, the specific article is used as a cohesive device to carry information about a previously mentioned noun.

What Makes a Noun Definite?

For a singular count noun, "a" or "an" becomes "the." For a plural or non-count noun, ("O") becomes "the." Apply the guidelines to the exercises and memorize them.

1. **One of a kind, part of a series, or superlative:**   — . **sentence level**
     the best, the most, the worst
     the first, the third, the fourth

Exercise: *Look at the following sentences where the definite article is always used. Put in the correct article.*
1. George Washington was ____ first president of the U.S. and maybe one of _____ best.
2. The student from Vietnam was ___ smartest in the Chemistry class.
3. My father was born on ___ third day of ___ fourth month in ___ second year of WWI.
4. ___ most delicious food is cooked by people who care about taste and appearance.
5. When I took Biology 111 for ___ second time, I got an "A".

2. Second mention:

paragraph cohesion

The definite article is used after a noun has been introduced. Typically the writer introduces a subject with the indefinite article *a* and then switches to ***the***. The indefinite article will be used to mark this particular noun through the entire paragraph and continue throughout the composition. This is called *second mention*. It is a cohesive devise to carry information that has been introduced about a noun throughout a paragraph without repeating the information over and over.

An apple is on a table. **The** apple is from North Georgia. **The** apple is one of many varieties grown locally. **The** apple is waiting for you to eat!

Exercise 41: *Insert the correct articles in the following mini-paragraphs.* Notice after the subject is first mentioned, the definite article is used throughout the paragraph to refer to the introduced noun.

1. Chemistry 111 is required for most students who want to major in a medical field. ___ chemistry class has a lab that must be taken with ___ class. ___ chemistry class is the first of a series of chemistry classes for these majors.

2. A man wearing red socks and a purple hat got on a bus going downtown. ___ bus number was 16 Noble, and it often carried people from Little Five Points downtown. ___ man sat next ___ woman who also wore a purple hat. ___ man turned to ___ woman and asked her where she got her purple hat. ___ woman said, "You tell me where you got your red socks, and I will tell you where I got my purple hat!" ___ bus continued downtown.

3. Shared information: between the reader/writer or listener/speaker

sentence level
and paragraph cohesion

This is perhaps the most difficult concept to understand. Here is one way to explain the concept. If someone close to you says that he/she is going to go to **THE** store. Probably you will know what store the person is going to. However, if the same person says that he/she is going to **A** store, you would probably ask, "What store?" Look at the cartoon.

62

4. Followed by a prepositional phrase or clause that makes the noun unique:

sentence level and paragraph cohesion

NOUN (+preposition + object): **The** love **(of my life)** is great!

NOUN (+clause): **The** man **(who got on the bus)** is famous.

When you decide whether to use the definite article in this case, you have to look beyond the noun to see if there is any prepositional phrase or clause which modifies the noun. Then you have to go back and put in the correct article. Look at the following exercise which contrasts nouns that are definite with nouns that are indefinite.

Exercise 42: *Put in the correct articles or O for no article.*
1. ___ broom is used in every clean house.
2. ___ broom that I used to sweep the kitchen got wet from the water on the floor.
3. ___ Cats sleep most of the day.
4. ___ cat on the sofa is sleeping where it is not supposed to.
5. ___ Volcanic eruptions can cause a lot of damage to people and crops.
6. ___ eruption of Mt. St. Helens spread ash over a 200-square-mile area.
7. ___ ESL student must take a placement test before registering for classes.
8. ___ ESL students from Taiwan often have a high level of grammar knowledge.
9. Police often give ___ parking tickets to students who park illegally.
10. ___ ticket that I got for speeding cost me my license.

5. Objects inside a space:

sentence level and paragraph cohesion

When you describe objects inside an enclosed space, they become definite because they are now different from other objects since they occupy a particular space. This applies to objects inside rooms, stores, cars, houses, and other spaces. Imagine that you are in your car. Turn your head and look at **THE** back seat, **THE** back door, and **THE** outside mirror.

Exercise 43: *Put in the definite articles in front of the nouns that are enclosed by a space.*

1. My friend bought an old house in an inner city neighborhood. At first he thought that he could live in the house "as is." Soon he found out that ___ water heater leaked and ___ hot water was brown. Then he discovered that ___ floor was rotten. ___ floor had to be replaced down to the sub-floor. ___ bathroom needed a new sink, and ___ drain was plugged up. Many windows were broken, and ___ heater needed a new thermostat. Finally my friend moved out of his "new house" and totally renovated it.

2 . The equipment for a modern classroom has changed in the last ten years. Now ___ overhead projector stands in the corner waiting to be used. The massive TV screen and VCR with wires going into ___ outlets take up a large portion of ___ classroom. ___ chalk and ___ blackboard have not been replaced but have become just one of many teaching tools.

Exercise 44: *Practice with definite articles. Give one reason from the above five for each of the definite articles used in this paragraph. The first one is completed for you.*

(1) **The food** in our refrigerator mostly consists of spicy homemade cooked food. Most of (2) **the food** that we eat is our Eritrean cultural food. (3) **The first shelf** of our refrigerator is filled with beverages such as vitamin D milk, Sunny Delight Orange Juice, and other caffeinated drinks that energizes members in our family after their visit to (4) **the refrigerator.** (5) **The second shelf** of our refrigerator contains homemade food in different containers with labels such as lasagna, macaroni and cheese, prepared salad, and other dishes as well. (6) **The third shelf** of our refrigerator includes veggies of (7) **the week** and fruit. This shelf has a variety of fruits and vegetables of different colors. Our refrigerator also has two divided sections on (8) **the bottom.** These sections hold lemons and tomatoes and my mother's favorite, jalepeno peppers. (9) **The door** of our refrigerator has three sections. (10) **The first level** includes our vitamins and prescriptions. (11) **The second level** is for different types of cheeses and sandwich spreads such as ketchup, mayonnaise, yellow mustard, jelly, peanut butter, and butter. Finally our third level of (12) **the refrigerator door** includes (13) **the salad.** If you have some time, please come and join me and my family for a delicious meal that you will never forget for (14) **the rest** of your life.

– Eden Anenia

1. *noun followed by a prepositional phrase*   8.
2.   9.
3.   10.
4.   11.
5.   12.
6.   13.
7   14.

Exercise 45: *Underline the nouns in the following passage and insert the articles (a, an, the) where needed. Then put the classification of the noun below.*

Yesterday I went into <u>store</u> and saw man trying on large hat. For security reasons, this store had closed-circuit TV system, and man was looking at image of himself on TV monitor. Later I saw same man in restaurant across street. He asked for piece of pie and cup of tea. They were out of tea, so customer ordered milk. All in all, it was strange day watching man with funny hat.

Example **store** *Type of noun:* singular, indefinite. *Article choice:* a.

	Type of noun	**Article choice**
1. man	_____	_____
2. hat	_____	_____
3. store	_____	_____
4. system	_____	_____
5. image	_____	_____
6. monitor	_____	_____
7. man	_____	_____
8. restaurant	_____	_____
9. street	_____	_____
10. piece	_____	_____
11. pie	_____	_____
12. cup	_____	_____
13. tea	_____	_____
14. tea	_____	_____
15. customer	_____	_____
16. milk	_____	_____
17. day	_____	_____
18. man	_____	_____
19. hat	_____	_____

Exercise 46: *Read the first paragraph. All the nouns are underlined and classified. The reasons are given for the choice of articles. After studying the first paragraph, read the next three paragraphs. Underline the nouns and put in the correct articles. This essay was written by Shintaro Fukada.*

Topic: ***What do you like or dislike about a job that you have or have had in the past?***

     I worked at a fruit <u>shop</u> for three <u>years</u> in <u>Japan</u>. Taking care of <u>fruit</u> is a very tough <u>job</u> because <u>fruit</u> is raw <u>food</u>. <u>Fruit</u> can be spoiled, so we, the <u>workers</u> in the fruit <u>shop</u>, had to be very careful. Of course, there are many <u>things</u> that make us happy to work at the fruit <u>shop</u>. <u>Fruit</u> is not just a <u>food</u>. We can enjoy the <u>smell</u> and <u>shape</u> of <u>fruit</u>, so I liked working at the fruit <u>shop</u>. However, it was one of the hardest <u>jobs</u> that I've ever experienced.

Nouns	Type of noun	Definite	Article chosen
1. shop	singular count	no, first mention	a
2. years	plural count	no	determiner-three
3. Japan	proper	yes	none
4. fruit	non-count	no	none
5. job	singular count	no	a
6. fruit	non-count	no	none
7. food	non-count	no	none
8. Fruit	(same as #4)	no	none
9. workers	plural count	yes, followed by prep. phrase	the
10. shop	singular count	yes, second mention	the
11. things	plural count	no	determiner-many
12. shop	singular count	yes, second mention	the
13. Fruit	(same as #4,6)	no	none
14. food	(same as #5)	no	none
15. smell and shape	singular count	yes, followed by prep. phrase	the
16. fruit	(same as #4,6,11)	no	none
17. shop	(same as #10)	yes, second mention	the
18. jobs	plural count	yes, superlative	the

Directions: Underline all nouns and put in the correct articles.

I had to wake up at six a.m. every morning when I was working at fruit shop because long distance trucks brought fruit early every morning. I made coffee for them and waited on them. And then I brought fruit from trucks to big refrigerator in our shop. To work at fruit shop, muscles are required. People do not notice this, but power is most important element to work at fruit shop. I am not powerful man, so it killed me every morning. (9 articles)

There was much joy working there. One of best things that always gave me joy was smell of fruit. Scent of fruit is totally different from any other scent. It is better than Chanel No. 5. Fruit shop was founded in 1965, so fruit shop absorbed scent of fruit for more than 25 years. Especially big refrigerator of fruit absorbed scent a lot. My favorite refrigerator was refrigerator of oranges. I sometimes cried in refrigerator of oranges, not because of sorrow, but because of joy. Whenever I talked about it, people doubted that scent of oranges could cause that much joy. Please trust me on this. It is best pleasure I have ever experienced. (12 articles)

In addition, my homeown is famous for peaches. Peaches of my hometown are best in Japan. When I came to Atlanta and found out that Georgia is also state of peaches, I felt destiny. I thought that coming to Atlanta was predetermined. I am man of peaches. I love peaches. (3 articles)

Scent of fruit always helps me to survive whenever I am in trouble. When I am in trouble, I imagine scent of fruit. It gives me relief. Thank you fruit. (2 articles)

Prepositions:

*When I started writing, I was not sure which prepositions to use. In the class I learned how to use the correct propositions. The teacher used a good and simple system. We had to write the nine most common prepositions on a note card. The nine most common prepositions are **at, by, for, from, in, of, on, to,** and **with**. By looking at these prepositions, I was able most likely to find the correct preposition. This system improved my use of prepositions. I will use this system in the next English class.*

– Rolf Fischer

The other mistake I partially corrected was using prepositions. Using prepositions in English is different than in my language. Whenever I was in confusion about which preposition to use, I would think in Serbo-Croatian and just translate the preposition into English. Although I have improved a lot, I still make mistakes. At last, I've changed the way of thinking. That means that now I always ask myself, "What preposition would an American put here?" The frustration caused by using wrong prepositions was even worse than not using articles correctly. Usually people wouldn't understand me at all, and I did not know how else I could change the meaning of the sentence. I partially corrected this by carefully listening to conversations and trying to memorize the expressions I would hear.

– Minja B.

Prepositions

Prepositions are very difficult for ESL students. There are several reasons.

1. There are more prepositions in English than other languages, and many prepositions in English have similar meanings such as *by*, *next to*, and *near*.

2. Prepositions in English do not necessarily translate into other languages, and one preposition in another language might translate into several prepositions in English.

3. Preposition use is often very unpredictable and specific to a certain context or expression.

Many ESL textbooks either ignore prepositions or spend very little time explaining them or providing exercises in spite of overwhelming evidence that misuse of prepositions is a serious problem. Ironically, preposition misuse is one of the errors that is not always self-correcting. The following explanations and exercises are designed to help "focus" on prepositions. By becoming aware of their use, accuracy will improve.

Prepositions are used in several different ways. They appear in prepositional phrases. They are connected to verbs and used to change the meaning of the verbs. They are also used in idiomatic phrases which are hard to quantify and predict. Misuse includes using them in front of adverbs and incorrectly with transitive verbs. This section on prepositions is designed to provide practice and understanding.

Look over this list of common prepositions. Be sure that you can recognize them when you see them. Think about the meaning of each as you scan this list.

aboard	below	in	through
about	beneath	inside	throughout
above	beside	into	to
across	besides	like	toward
*after	between	near	under
against	beyond	of	underneath
along	by	off	*until
among	down	on	up
around	during	out	upon
as	except	over	with
at	*for	past	within
*before	from	*since	without
behind			

*These prepositions can be used as subordinating conjunctions if followed by a subject and a verb. The preposition "for" can be used as a coordinating conjunction.

Prepositional Phrases

Prepositions are most often attached to a noun. This is called a prepositional phrase (P + object = prepositional phrase). It is very important to be able to recognize prepositional phrases. It is also very easy to learn how to recognize them.

Example: The book is (**on the table**).
The computer is (**on the desk**) (**near the table**) (**in the library**).

Exercise 47: *Read the short paragraph and underline the prepositional phrases. Circle the prepositions. Try to work fast, but accurately.*

The cat sits in the window on the ledge facing toward the sun. She sits there all during the day soaking up the sun. When the light and heat shift to another spot, she moves her body along the path of the rays of the sun. The only movement on the cat's body is the silent jumping of the fleas on her skin invisible to all but the cat. When the sun moves on, the cat jumps from the window ledge to find another spot in the house or the yard. This is the life of a cat. What a life!

Exercise 48: *Find a short article in the newspaper. Read it carefully and underline all prepositional phrases. Work quickly. Read the prepositional phrases out loud. Do this often. It will help!*

Phrasal Prepositions

Most prepositions are one word, but some consist of more than one word and are called phrasal prepositions. Phrasal prepositions are used frequently in both spoken and written communication. Here is a list of the common phrasal prepositions.

because of	in case of	in spite of	on account of
by way of	instead of	in lieu of	on the side of

Exercise 49: *Use the above phrasal prepositions in a sentence. Make up sample sentences very quickly and listen to the sound of the prepositions.*

Phrasal Verbs or Two-Word Verbs

Prepositions are used with verbs to alter the meaning slightly. For example, you can agree **to** something and agree **with** somebody. ESL students have to be aware of how prepositions can change the meaning of the verb and the sentence.

Exercise 50: *Put the correct preposition(s) after each verb. If there are more prepositions than one, think of how they change meaning.*

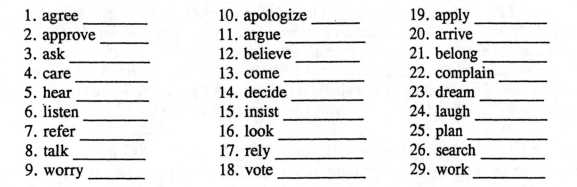

1. agree _____	10. apologize _____	19. apply _____
2. approve _____	11. argue _____	20. arrive _____
3. ask _____	12. believe _____	21. belong _____
4. care _____	13. come _____	22. complain _____
5. hear _____	14. decide _____	23. dream _____
6. listen _____	15. insist _____	24. laugh _____
7. refer _____	16. look _____	25. plan _____
8. talk _____	17. rely _____	26. search _____
9. worry _____	18. vote _____	29. work _____

Exercise 51: *Read the following paragraph. Underline all the two-word verbs.*

Two-word verbs create a level of informality in the English language. Many Asian languages have different vocabulary to indicate the levels of formality. For example, the Korean language has five levels including intimate, familiar or informal, polite, formal, and honorific. These levels create a highly stratified language with words and grammar depending on the social relationship among the speakers. In English one indication of formality is word choice. Two-word verbs tend to indicate an informal, oral tone to the English language. Teenagers say that they hang out with their friends; professionals associate with other people. You can think about a major purchase or consider whether or not to buy it. You can talk about a problem with your friends or discuss it with your professors. You can ask your friend for a favor but request a book through interlibrary loan. In most cases there is a word that is similar in meaning to most two-words verbs, but the word is considered more formal. Adding to (expanding) your vocabulary in this area will help you out (advance your knowledge).

Nine Most Common Prepositions:
at, by, for, from, in, of, on, to, with

These are the nine prepositions which are used the most. Native speakers have a mental inventory of prepositions and check off a list when searching for the right preposition to use. This mental list consists of most of the nine prepositions. A native speaker will go through the list searching for the right preposition until he/she "hears" the correct one. This is an advanced kind of guessing.

Most ESL students do not have this list of prepositions in their heads. A teacher may say to an ESL student, "This preposition is wrong, so try another preposition." Usually the ESL student can not think of another preposition to try and is stuck.

In addition, teachers do not encourage ESL students *to guess*. But eventually students will have to build on a **feeling** of what is right and wrong by guessing. More practice with prepositions will increase a student's sense of what preposition is correct.

Exercise 52: *List the nine most common prepositions on a 3x5 index card. Put this card in your dictionary or some place handy where you can refer to it when you need to choose a preposition. Use this card to "guess" by substituting prepositions from the list in your own writing. You will probably "hear" the right prepositions as you go down the list. Use this preposition card to find the right prepositions in the exercises on the next page.*

```
┌─────────────────────────┐
│      Nine Most          │
│  Common Prepositions    │
│          at             │
│          by             │
│          for            │
│          from           │
│          in             │
│          of             │
│          on             │
│          to             │
│          with           │
└─────────────────────────┘
```

Exercise 53: *The following exercise will help establish a list of prepositions and give you practice using the same process that native speakers use "to find and hear" the right preposition. Use the preposition card to help you "guess."*

1. All ___ all, the students did well ___ the honors history class.
2. ___ conclusion, everyone had a good time ___ the party.
3. The owner put the new house up ___ sale ___ the first ___ the month.
4. ___ case of emergency, press down ___ the red button.
5. ___ the one hand, there is much to be said for working and attending college ___ the same time.
6. ___ the other hand, going to school full-time gives a student more time to study and concentrate.
7. Beginning ESL students often translate readings word ___ word.
8. ___ best, this is only a temporary victory ___ the whole game.
9. ___ the moment, the student is ___ danger ___ losing "A" average.
10. The teacher said Saed was ___ far the best tennis player ___ the class.

***

11. All ___ a sudden, the car stopped quickly ___ front ___ me.
12. ___ the way, did you remember to pay the electric bill last month?
13. What is the matter ___ Jim? He seems very tired all ___ the time.
14. Should the students begin a test as soon as they get it? ___ all means, the sooner they start, the more time they have to write.
15. This pen spills ink all over. ___ that case, don't put it ___ your purse!
16. Were you able to make use ___ the exercises that I showed you last Wednesday?
17. The foreign student advisor said that I had to take ___ least twelve credits a semester.
18. I'm sorry, but I don't have anything ___ mind to suggest ___ your successful career.
19. ___ the event ___ an emergency, call the hospital immediately.
20. The teacher never comes ___ the point and wanders ___ the topic all the time.

***

21. I haven't been able to get ___ touch ___ my teacher all week.
22. ___ the most part, she did well ___ the essay and multiple choice parts ___ the test.
23. That car in the used car lot is ___ sale. Are you interested ___ it?
24. Aren't you glad that you went to the wedding party ___ us ___ all?
25. The teacher suggested that we learn the two article rules ___ heart.
26. They are going to go to California ___ way ___ Montana and Washington state.
27. Many students work ___ night ___ order to earn extra money to buy books.
28. That was my e-mail address last quarter. Now it is out ___ date this quarter.
29. Thrifty students often use newspapers to cover books ___ place ___ bought book covers.
30. Try to complete all ___ the questions ___ that page ___ your own memory.

Extra Prepositions

Often students will put prepositions in where they aren't needed. This mistake is just as serious as using the wrong preposition. This usually happens in two completely different situations. Read about both of them. Look over your writing and see if you make either one of these mistakes. If you do, you will have to understand the grammar that is involved, so you can correct the preposition errors.

1. There are a group of adverbs that are often mistaken for nouns. When this happens, the adverbs are used incorrectly as objects in prepositional phrases. Below is a list of some of these adverbs:

here	inside
there	outside
everywhere	uptown
	downtown

Incorrect: Many people have gone to downtown.
Correct: Many people have gone downtown.

Incorrect: Restaurants have patios for customers to eat in there.
Correct: Restaurants have patios for customers to eat there.

Be Careful! Sometimes these same words are used as adjectives. In the prepositional phrase, *in the downtown area, downtown* is an adjective which modifies the noun *area*.

Exercise 54: *Cross out the extra prepositions in the following paragraphs.*

City planners are currently discussing the revitalization of the downtown areas. One of the plans is to convert offices in downtown to residential lofts. These lofts could be converted in everywhere there is space above storefronts and old abandoned office buildings. Even in the city of Atlanta, this effort is gaining support in here. Recently Georgia State University has joined the effort and begun to move the campus further in downtown using old offices as learning spaces. The transformation of the Rialto Theater as a performing arts center and music department is one example.

The problem of maintaining architectural integrity within the city has surfaced. Georgia State University currently wants to tear down several old buildings in the core of the city and rebuild from in the inside to in the outside. Many preservationists claim this plan would destroy the historic architecture and displace some of the vital existing businesses. These controversial questions are surfacing in everywhere where revitalization efforts are underway. Regardless of what happens, most people are delighted about a renewed interest in the inner city.

2. Inserting a preposition incorrectly with a transitive verb or leaving out a preposition with an intransitive verb.

Transitive verbs are followed by a direct object (S+V+O).

Intransitive verbs are followed by no object but often a prepositional phrase (S+V or S+V+PP).

Unfortunately, many verbs in English can be both transitive and intransitive.

For example: I cooked soup yesterday for lunch. *(transitive verb)*

I cook in the morning and afternoon. *(intransitive verb followed by a PP)*

Often students incorrectly add a preposition after a transitive verb.

Incorrect: We asked to the mechanic to fix our car.

Correct: We asked the mechanic to fix our car.

Or students leave out a preposition after an intransitive verb.

Incorrect: I walked the block.

Correct: I walked around the block.

If you make this error, learn how to check in the dictionary to see if a verb is transitive or intransitive. Intransitive verbs are marked *int. or vi.* and transitive verbs are marked *tran. or vt.*

Exercise 55: *Look up the following verbs in the dictionary and indicate whether they are transitive or intransitive or both. Also read the definitions of the verbs.*

	Transitive	Intransitive	Both
1. agree	_____	_____	_____
2. exit	_____	_____	_____
3. run	_____	_____	_____
4. apply	_____	_____	_____
5. procrastinate	_____	_____	_____

Exercise 56: *Put in the correct prepositions in the following exercise.*

"In," "on," and "at" are the three prepositions that most grammar textbooks discuss _____ detail. These prepositions are the easiest to discuss because they reflect a pattern _____ the most general _____ the specific in both time and space. For example, when you are referring _____ a location, you start _____ the most general and move _____ the specific when using "in," "on," and "at." I live **in** Atlanta **on** Highland Avenue **at** house number 555. The same order can be applied when describing time _____ the general _____ the specific. I was born **in** December **on** the 15th day **at** 2:30 am. Unfortunately, it is very rare _____ students to

75

encounter this general to specific order ____ either their own writing or ____ typical academic writing. Even this rule for preposition use can be applied ____ only limited situations. However students can increase the accuracy ____ prepositions by consciously listening ____ them, highlighting them ____ reading materials, and ____ becoming aware ____ what kind ____ preposition errors that they make.

Exercise 57: *Replace the incorrect prepositions, put in prepositions where needed, and take out unnecessary prepositions.*

(1) Many people have gone to downtown to watch parades ever since they were children. (2) Often on these special days, the stores in the downtown area are open long hours. (3) In some cities the department stores have considered about special parade days with sales both on inside the store and on outside the store. (4) Often the merchants display merchandise in outside under umbrellas. (5) Now it is popular about restaurants to have outside seating. (6) City governments are now talking closing the streets to cars and creating open malls on the streets. (7) This new trend is a way to increase to a sense of new community and the new "walking city." (8) Soon in downtown will look like the small town squares of days gone by. (9) Suburbanites who have to drive everywhere to make even the smallest purchases will flock toward to the city center to enjoy the feeling of the hustle and bustle of the city. (10) A rebirth of city activities and city centers is already taking place within the country.

Exercise 58: *Take out unnecessary prepositions, add prepositions, and change incorrect prepositions in the following paragraph. There are six errors.*

More and more students are registering in by themselves using computers. Advisors meet on students year round to help plan programs of study and prepare students to transfer to other schools. One of the easiest ways to plan your college courses is to look with the college catalog. Listing all the courses and the majors, this one resource is available to students upon admission to the college. Unfortunately, many students don't seek help before registering classes. As a result, many students end with many courses that they did not need to take, thereby lengthening their college stay. Students will often become aware in gaps in needed course work just before transferring or graduating. Most colleges have shifted from a mandatory advising process to one which is totally voluntary. Be sure that you have planned on your schedule carefully before you register.

Gerunds and Infinitives
The Traditional Explanation
Bolinger's Theory
Exercises

JOHN STOPPED SMOKING.

JOHN STOPPED TO SMOKE.

Infinitives and Gerunds – the Traditional Explanation

Almost all ESL students have seen the example contrasting gerunds and infinitives used after a verb.

John stopped smoking and
John stopped to smoke.

This example is used by teachers because it points out the difference in meaning when you use a gerund as opposed to an infinitive. For students the choice of a gerund or an infinitive is a big problem. Teachers and grammar books recommend memorizing three lists of verbs. One list is verbs which tend to take the infinite form. The second list is verbs which tend to take the gerund. The third list is verbs which can take either.

List of Verbs followed by Infinitives	List of Verbs followed by Gerunds	List of Verbs followed by Infinitives OR Gerunds
decide	appreciate	begin
expect	avoid	like
forget	can't help	love
hope	consider	hate
learn	discuss	can't stand
need	enjoy	start
offer	finish	stop
plan	go	try
promise	keep	
refuse	mind	
seem	postpone	
try	practice	
wait	quit	
want	regret	
would like	think about	

Exercise 59: *Use the lists above and choose either a gerund or an infinitive.*

1. The students wanted _____ (graduate) with honors from college.
2. If you postpone _____ (pay) your income tax, you will pay a penalty.
3. The parents considered _____ (turn) off the television during the week days.
4. Students should think about _____ (transfer) after completing the core requirements.
5. Don't stop _____ (water) your plants during the winter season.

Memorizing the three lists of verbs is tough. The likelihood that students will come up with the right infinitive or gerund by searching their memory in the middle of writing an essay s slim. This solution leads to the frequent question and admission, "Teacher, does this verb take an infinitive or a gerund? I forget."

Bolinger's Theory

Grammarian Dwight Bolinger suggests a semantic approach to the choice of an infinitive or gerund. He says that the writer should consider the meaning of the verb and make a choice based on the following generalizations.

1. **Positive and negative connotations:**

    A. Gerunds tend to follow negative or pessimistic verbs, including the following verbs such as *deny, avoid, regret, and refuse*

    B. Infinitives tend to follow positive or optimistic verbs, including the following verbs such as *hope, promise, love, and want*

2. **Completed and uncompleted actions/real and hypothetical situations**

    A. Gerunds tend to follow verbs which are real, vivid, and fulfilled or completed such as *keep, finish and recall.*

    B. Infinitives tend to follow verbs which are hypothetical, in the future, or unfulfilled/not completed such as *expect, hope, offer, and seem.*

Look at the following examples:

Gerund – negative implication
She denied losing the money.
I avoided making any decision until I was ready to pay the total amount for the computer.
They regretted going to California last summer because of the torrential rains.

Infinitive – positive implication
I hope to return to my country for the New Year celebrations.
I promise to help you the next time you are in trouble.
I love to study where I can look out the window.

Gerund – completed action
I finally finished typing my research paper for the English class.
John kept trying the software program again and again until it worked.

Infinitive – uncompleted action
The used car dealer offered to fix the car that she just bought.
The rain seems to have stopped altogether.

Note: For a further discussion see "Infinitives and Gerunds" in *The Grammar Book: An ESL//EFL Teacher's Course* (1983) by Marianne Celce-Murcia and Diane Larsen-Freeman.

Exercise 60: *Use these general semantic rules to choose between a gerund or an infinitive in the following sentences and test Bolinger's theory.*

> *Gerunds = negative and completed   Infinitives = positive and uncompleted*

1. _____ That person really resents (to take, taking) ESL classes.
2. _____ Please stop (to chew, chewing) gum and blowing bubbles.
3. _____ The chemistry teacher claims (to be, being) an expert in lab instruction.
4. _____ His student assistant failed (to include, including) all the papers on the final exam.
5. _____ I hesitate (to say, saying) anything to correct his speech.
6. _____ The students don't plan (to leave, leaving) until they get their final grades.
7. _____ Those workers deny (to know, knowing) anything about the new plans.
8. _____ Did the violinists practice (to use, using) their new bows in the orchestra?
9. _____ The students didn't dare (to suggest, suggesting) the possibility of a take-home exam.
10. _____ I would appreciate (to hear, hearing) from you when you receive my package.

***

1. _____ Most students avoid (to study, studying) subjects that they are not interested in even if the subjects relate to their majors.
2. _____ The Department of Transportation refused (to consider, considering) bike paths as a traffic alternative.
3. _____ Are you going to suggest (to travel, traveling) by train to California?
4. _____ I can't stand (to wait, waiting) in line at the bookstore when the quarter begin.
5. _____ The teacher hesitated (to remind, reminding) the student of her absences.
6. _____ Our guests don't plan (to leave, leaving) until they have seen all the sights.
7. _____ Did you offer (to translate, translating) those medical documents for your friend?
8. _____ Have you begun (to write, writing) your first literary criticism?
9. _____ Did the real estate agent offer (to buy, buying) their vacation home?
10. _____ I can't stand (to wait, waiting) for people who are late for dinner.

Note: Accuracy in choosing whether to use a gerund or an infinitive improves with practice. Examine the written material around you. Also you might consider whether your first language has both gerunds and infinitives and how they are used.

Transformational Exercises

These exercises are great for practicing changes in verbs, nouns, and adding articles. They may not guarantee perfect grammar in your compositions and essays, but they do help you to remember the grammar basics.

Exercise 61: *You are to do two things to this paragraph. First, change the nouns (example:* students) *from plural to singular. Second, change the time focus of the paragraph from the past tense to the present tense. When you make these changes, you will also have to change adjectives and verbs for agreement, and you have to add appropriate articles. This is not an easy exercise. Be sure to check your work with other students in the class to see what you missed, or what they missed.*

It was 3 a.m. All things on the university campus seemed ghostlike in the quiet, misty darkness – except for the computer center. There were the students, rumpled and bleary-eyed, looking at their computer screens and tapping away at the keys. With their eyes on their screens, they tapped on the keys for hours. Like gamblers, these students were pursuing obsessions that overshadowed all parts of their lives. These students were compulsive computer programmers, working without breaks. They were irresistibly drawn there. They were there because they wanted to be there.

Exercise 62: *Now change everything in this paragraph that is singular to plural and everything that is in the present to the past.*

An ESL writing student takes particular care to write her essay thoughtfully. She develops her thesis, organizes her ideas, and begins to write her introduction – all in the first fifteen minutes. Then, she methodically writes her first draft, checking for agreement and correct vocabulary. She remembers to do it this way for every homework assignment. She wants to do well so that she can pass the class. The good news is that she does!

Exercise 63: *Change this paragraph to the present tense and the nouns to singular..*

Alarm clocks rang while tired children looked vaguely out their windows. It was still dark outside, and cool morning breezes filled the small dark rooms of these sleepy students. Houses were quiet and still as students had to face the adventures and mysteries of first days of school. Their hearts were pumping so fast that it took no time at all to pull on jeans and sweatshirts. Soon, they were ready to go, and their adventures were about to begin

Exercise 64: *Now in this paragraph change everything that is singular to plural and everything that is in the present verb tense to the past.*

There is a leisure boom that is happening in Japan offering relief to both the Japanese worker and the Japanese student. A Japanese worker labors about 200 more hours per year than an American worker. With school in session every weekday plus Saturday morning, a Japanese student has almost 60 more class days than an American student. One company requires each employee to take a longer vacation, and another company is eliminating the traditional Saturday workday. Every school is considering cutting back the hours of study to offer some more leisure time for younger students in Japan.

Section Four: Writing Samples

Samples One – Four: Timed Writing Samples and Exercises
Samples Five – Eight: Edited Essays with Anlyses
Samples Nine – Twelve: Revised, Out-of-Class Essays

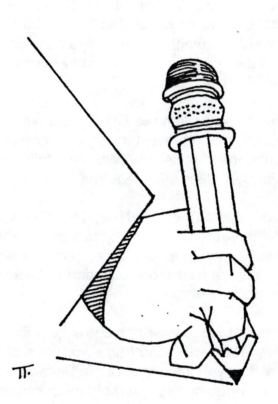

Writing Samples

The following are essays written by students in ESL Advanced Writing classes. The student writers represent a variety of countries and continents, and we have chosen samples from Asian, African, and European student writers.

The twelve papers fall into three broad categories and represent a range of writing that we see in our advanced ESL classes. The first paper is a handwritten paper written in a timed-writing (90-minute) situation. This essay displays the kinds of changes and corrections that students make in their papers as they write and edit.

The next three papers (Samples Two, Three, and Four) also represent in-class, timed writing that tends to be somewhat "rough" (i.e., may contain grammatical mistakes or awkward wording) and less developed than out-of-class, revised papers. Following these essays are a few brief questions that encourage you to analyze the essays further.

The next four papers (Samples Five, Six, Seven, and Eight) are all models of Example essays, and they represent in-class writing that has been edited after the teacher has recommended revisions. We have followed these essays with a brief commentary about their distinctive features.

The last four papers (Samples Nine, Ten, Eleven, and Twelve) are revised essays that students wrote for out-of-class assignments. The essays are longer, more developed and to some extent, more carefully written. The last paper of this group, a literary essay, shows the application of basic writing principles to a paper that uses primary documentation.

These samples of student writing show how ESL students respond to given topics and develop ideas within the framework of a structured essay. The basic parts of the essay that you learned about in Section One are represented, including hooks, thesis statements, body paragraphs with support, and conclusions. These essays are part of a copyrighted document. No part should be used for any purpose except in quoted form with credit given to the author(s).

Sample One – Timed Writing (90 Minutes)

Note: *Sample One is a copy of a student's handwritten essay. This essay was a departmental writing exit, in which the student was given the topic at the beginning of 90 minutes. This essay shows some of the corrections and changes that students make while they write. This essay was written by Herrick Ding.*

Topic: *Contrast what you thought college would be like before you started with what you now know it to be like.*

I Was Wrong

The ~~edu~~ education system of America is very different from ~~my country~~ the education system of my country, Taiwan. During the ~~t~~ time when I studied in National Taipei Institute of Technology, my classmates and I used to study only one or two days before every ~~test~~ test. We didn't care what grade we would get. We only cared that we would pass the classes or not, and ~~that I was~~ every college student did it in my country. Therefore, before I came to the United States to study, I thought I would do the same way in a college in America. However, every thing ~~was~~ was totally different when I went to a college in America.

~~The biggest differents differences are~~
Now, I am getting better in my school. I think

85

that I have to do homework and to study after every

class and I must study every subject and ~~detail~~ detail

by myself are the biggest and the most important

differences.

In addition, the teachers in my country teach
                                    detail
the students every ~~detail~~ that is in the textbooks, but
                             only   the
the teachers in America ~~teach~~ teach students the concepts.
                          the
I only studied what ~~the~~ teachers ~~too~~ (tought) in the

classes, and I never had to find any information to

support what I learn from the teachers when

I studied ~~too~~ in my country. ~~when~~ Now, I

have to study every ~~detail~~ detail by myself and

~~to~~ find a lot of information to help me ~~to~~

understand the textbooks. In the beginning, it

was very hard for me to adjust to this ~~out~~

styles of studying and teaching. Now, I think

that is very good for me to really understand

what the teachers teach and what I learn.
                                              that
In short, ~~I~~ it was wrong that I thought ~~that~~ going

to a college ● was a very easy for me. Studying

and learning take time, and I have to concentrate

on my classes and to do my best. There is

86

nothing I can do but studing hard if I want
to really get knowledge and technology from a
college.

While I was studying in National Taipei Institute
of Technology, my classmates and I copied
homework from each other in order to have time
to go to the movies, to go dancing, or to go to
countryside. We didn't study before the day
of every test because it was easy to pass
in the first quarter
the classes. However, when I went to Dekalb College,
I recognized that I couldn't do the same way in
America because I would fail the classes. Unlike
the teachers in my country, the teachers in America
ask the students to do their homework by themselves
and assign a assignment after every class. Therefore
I have to study and do my homework every day.
I only can relax on the weekend. Nevertheless,
I do believe I can learn alot from my
teachers and classes, and I think that is the reason
why I go to the school in America.

Sample Two – Timed Writing (90 Minutes)

Topic: *What advice do you have for someone who needs to save time during his/her daily schedule?*

I am lucky to know my best friend, Mandy, in America. She is competent in many things. She has a full time job during the daytime, and she studies a computer course at night. On weekend, she works for her church. In addition, she takes care of her nephews all the time because her nephews' mother died several years ago. Because she needs to be concerned about all things that I describe above, she is a very busy person. She doesn't have enough time to sleep everyday. I hope that I can help her, so I want to give her two advice to save her time.

I suggest her to make a daily schedule. A daily schedule is very useful for her to arrange her time. She should make a daily schedule for next day before she go to bed at night. The most important thing is to practice the schedule that she made at night, and not to change the schedule carelessly. I think this schedule can help her to save her time. For example, she can depend one her schedul to decide how much time she spends for each thing. She also can plan and organize her things well.

Moreover, I suggest that she should learn how to say "no" to people. Because she is very kind and generous person, she seldom rejects people when they ask her for help. Therefore, she always has many extra things to do beside her schedule. I always tell Mandy that sometimes to say "no" is not a bad thing, and that people can have more chances to learn how to handle their businesses, and also Mandy can save her time.

To make a daily schedul for next day, and to learn how to say "no" to people are the two important things to save Mandy's time. Also, she should learn the two things at the same time because saying "no" to people is a necessary way to keep her to her daily schedule. I hope that she can accept my advice, and she can arrange her time more better than now she does.

– Fang Yi Hsu (351 words)

Directions for Analysis:

It's a good practice to analyze essays after reading them. Here are some ideas for analysis. First, underline the thesis of the essay. Use the margins to block off the parts of the essay: the introduction, the body paragraphs, the conclusion. Next, see if you can identify the strategies for the introduction and the conclusion. Then, take a few minutes and answer the questions that follow.

Writing Considerations:

1. How is the paper organized?

_____

2. How does the student "personalize" the topic?

_____

3. What kind of introduction strategy does the student use?

_____

4. Is this introduction good, fair, or poor?

_____

Grammatical Considerations:

1. What is the time frame of the essay?

_____

2. What verb tense is used most frequently?

_____

3. What "non-English" expressions can you find?

_____

4. What kinds of noun problems and article omissions can you find?

_____

_____

Sample Three – Timed Writing (90 minutes)

Topic: *What skill do you wish you had?*

Right now, I am sitting in front of my computer, and I try to type the essay which is homework due on Monday. The typing process begins after I decide which topic to write about. But wait a minute, something does not look right in this picture. My eyes focus on the keyboard, and they try to find the appropriate keys. I feel like an eagle which is ready to strike its prey. Two of my fingers do the mechanical work of activating the keys. I definitely could not impress anyone with this slow and sluggish typing skill. I wish I had a speedy and accurate typing skill because it is a must in today's academic and professional world.

When my wife was in college, I saw that most of her work had to be typed. Towards her senior year her projects got longer and longer, and of course they were more time consuming. She typed her projects with lightening speed without looking at the keyboard and using all of her fingers. I was deeply impressed with her typing skills. Imagine this, if I have to type such projects, that would take me forever. I can understand that teachers want projects typed because I assume it is sometimes difficult to decipher personal handwriting.

In addition to academics, there is also a need for fast typing in the professional world. How would you act if you were an employer and read a handwritten resume? I think you would throw it in the trash can without business world. My previous job was more hands on and mainly out in the field, and for this reason I got away with my limited typing skills. I had to write

90

short and compact service reports for the customer which included the work I carried out and some recommendations for the future. My employer expected me to be out in the field and make money. In the future, I hope to work as a maintenance engineer in a power plant. There I would be responsible for coordinating the maintenance of the power plant equipment with their vendors. In this position a fast typing skill is a must. I could not afford to work on a single project for a long time because time is money.

For these reasons I would like to improve my typing skills, and I hope to break this barrier one day. I think I ignored this fact for a long time, but now it has caught up with me. My only solution would be probably to take a typing course to learn it the proper way.

– Rolf Fischer (443 words)

Writing Considerations:

1. What kind of introduction does the writer use?

_____

2. How does the support differ in each body paragraph?

_____

3. What kind of conclusion strategy does the student use?

_____

4. Is the conclusion good, fair, or poor and why?

_____

Grammatical Considerations:

1. How does the verb tense change from the introduction to the first body paragraph?

_____

_____

2. Complete a sentence analysis on paragraph 3. Does the writer show sufficient sentence variety? Why or why not?

_____

Sample Four – Timed Writing (90 minutes)

Topic: Describe the class that you had in high school that has helped you the most in college.

If someone is really concerned about your problems in school, he/she will be willing to help you to learn. I had difficulties in math when I was in middle school. I really hated math, and I didn't learn anything because I didn't understand the process. Then when I was in high school, I had a very good teacher. He saw my problems, and he offered to help me. He taught me many skills from the fundamental concepts to the advanced principles, so I learned from the basic skills to the high level in this class.

I took intermediate Algebra when I was in tenth grade in Vietnam. The class met in the morning three times per week for an hour. There were 20 students in this class. Mr. Hoan was my teacher. He was really good and kind to his students. He was especially concerned about me. After we had had a discussion, he understood the origin of my math difficulties. He wanted me to make progress in learning so he tried to help me learn.

I first had to learn the basic concepts from Mr. Hoan. He taught me from the beginning how to solve positive and negative numbers, fractions, absolute value, and equations. He made me study hard. I had to do a lot of homework every night. He taught me individually three hours per week. He was very patient with my math problems. He made flash cards to help me learn the math formulas. Sometimes he had to use visual aids or objects to help me understand the problems. I kept doing a lot of homework and getting help from Mr. Hoan, so mathematics began to get easier for me. I became more interested in math.

As my math skills developed, I got involved with my classmates to study in a group. My group had four people, and I became the best one in this group. I could solve the problems when my friends got stuck. I became more advanced in class and self confident. I could solve the problems on the board in front of my classmates and Mr. Hoan.

I realized that math class helped me to have basic skills and good grades in mathematics and is continuing to help me in college. While I have lived in America, I have attended math classes in college. I feel confident in class although my English is limited. Because I learned the basic skills, I could solve problems quickly and easily.

The math class that I took in tenth grade in high school helped me make progress in school although I had math difficulties in middle school. Thankfully, Mr. Hoan helped me and opened my mind. I feel more confident in college, and I can solve math problems without much trouble.

– Xuanthao Tran Ngo (463 words)

Writing Considerations:

1. Does a 6-paragraph organization work effectively in this essay? Why or why not?

_____

2. If not, do you see a better way to organize this essay? How?

_____

_____

3. How are the body paragraphs developed?

_____

4. Does the conclusion adequately complete or "finish" the essay?

_____

Grammatical Considerations:

1. What verb mistakes exist in paragraph 5?

_____

2. Are verb mistakes a chronic problem? _____

3. Complete a sentence analysis on paragraphs two and three. Do these sentence types create a "simple" and "choppy" effect?

_____

4. How can sentence variety be improved in paragraphs two and three?

_____

_____

Sample Five – Example

Topic: What kind of music do you prefer and why?

While I was sitting in my room, I moved into another passage. I saw myself dancing on a stage, and I remembered that it was my aunt's wedding ceremony. Some people came to the stage to shower me with money because I was dancing so beautifully. The music was what made the magic to me. Because of this event I considered Afrojuju music as the kind of music that I like most. It keeps me in contact with my roots, it is very informative, and it has a very natural sound.

Afrojuju music is a traditional form of music which originated from the western part of Nigeria called Oyo. The Oyomesis (the people of Oyo) were the original composers of this music. This was the music they played during occasions like birthdays, weddings, child naming ceremonies and traditional festivals. Because I am from Oyo and Afrojuju is my traditional music, it reminds me of my roots.

The lyrics of these songs is what makes the music very unique. The lyrics say a lot about either the ills or the good conducts of the society. It also tells us about the conduct of the society and age class. It tells us what the society expects of these classes. This enables me to keep my morals and social values.

The natural instruments which are used to make different sounds for this music make it stay conservative. This also helps keep its traditional sound preserved. Because these instruments are made from local products, they make the sound very different from modern musical instruments and other traditional types of music. The talking drum which is also known as "Gangan" is the instrument I like the most. It is made from animal skin and wood. The talking drum is one of the instruments that makes Afrojuju music different from other traditional kinds of music.

Well, I must admit that I believe no matter modernized the world is, the most natural form of things will always be the best. Afrojuju has always been a type of music that sounds very beautiful, native and natural, and I hope it will stay like that.

– Rafat Bello (354 words)

Analysis of Sample Five:

Sample Five begins with a flashback hook and has a traditional three part thesis as the concluding sentence of the introduction. Body paragraphs are developed with facts, as the student gives information that would be general knowledge to most Nigerians. Though paragraph three is minimally developed, there are sufficient details throughout to make the paper interesting. Verb tense, especially the use of passive voice, is used accurately. The paper ends with a prediction kind of conclusion.

Sample Six – Example

Topic: What skill do you wish you had?

As I was growing up, my mother sewed. She didn't make new clothes, but she always fixed the rips and tears on our old clothes. I remember her sitting in front of the sewing machine for many hours looking at our clothes and carefully mending them, until they looked almost perfect. She fixed the little hole in my jeans and in my brother's shorts. As we were growing older, we grew taller, and we needed larger sizes. My mother used to enjoy sewing and was happy whenever she could make nice clothes for us. I used to feel happy watching my mother sew, but I never had the chance to learn how to sew. Because sewing requires a lot of patience and is detailed oriented, it seemed like magic to me when I was little. Now it is time to learn how to sew, so I can save money.

Many kinds of skills need patience especially sewing. At first you have to choose a pattern and the type of material you want. Then if you find everything that you want, you must carefully cut out the pattern, and this takes a lot of time. To make sure that you have enough material, you must place the patterns on the material correctly. When this is done, then you can begin to sew. Patience is important, but so is an eye for detail.

Perhaps the one thing that makes you a good seamstress from a bad one is the eye for detail. It is important that you do things as correctly as possible and as neat as possible if you want clothes to look good. The more detail involved in the pattern, the more patience is required as well as the need to do detailed work. If you can be both patient and have an eye for detail, then you can save money by sewing your own clothes.

The ability to save money is a benefit of sewing. The better you become at sewing, the more money you can save. You no longer need to have other people repair your clothing any longer. You also don't have to buy expensive clothes from the stores.

I made a night gown that looked just like a big shirt. This was easy to make for a beginner. Sometimes my eyes hurt from the close work for doing and redoing to make things perfect. When I am finally finished, I feel so good. I am proud of myself. Now I am making a simple skirt, and I really enjoy sewing. My mother was such a skilled person, and I hope in the future I will be able to sew as well as my mother did.

– Ji-Su Song (450 words)

Analysis of Sample Six:

In **Sample Six,** the introduction is noticeably longer than any other paragraph in the essay. The hook is a well-developed anecdote (a past narrative), in which the student sets up the rationale for the skill she wants to have, sewing. In the body paragraphs, the student uses "you" when referring to any person. Sometimes, freshman composition instructors frown upon this informal usage and discourage any switches in points-of-view. The writer effectively supports her position by writing about the process of sewing that she learned from her mother. The conclusion (a result) suitably ends the essay.

Sample Seven – Example

Topic: *Do you function best in the morning, afternoon, or evening? Discuss your favorite time of day.*

"Gene – a single part of the material at the center (nucleus) of a cell, which controls the development of qualities in a living thing which have been passed on (inherited) from its parents."
Longman Dictionary of American English

Our natural biological clock depends on genes. We have written in our DNA material how much sleep we need, and what is the best time to do exercises. Some people try to put the natural clock of all people into a standard, but from the scientist's point of view, it is impossible because everybody is different. I do not have enough knowledge to talk about it, but I know that my body functions depend on the style of my living. There are times when I function the best during the day, and sometimes the best time to do something is in the middle of the night.

When I was in high school and I had to get up early, the best time to think and to do exercises was in the morning. I was really active and full of energy. My days finished very early. About nine in the evening I was very tired and I went to sleep. Since January I have very similar days like when I was in high school. I get up about five o'clock in the morning and I go to school. After classes I do some exercise like running, swimming, or playing tennis. When I come back, I am very, very tired. I am full of energy from early in the morning till 5 o'clock. After this time all I dream about is a bed and a good sleep.

There was a time in my life that days looked much different. After I graduated from high school, I have two years free. I worked, but it was only two hours a day and in the afternoon. Everyday when I finished my work, I went to the pub or the disco with my friends. I usually came back home about 1 o'clock at night. I could do it because I did not have to get up in the morning. At that time, my body functioned better in the night. During the day, I was lazy and tired, but at night I was full of energy. I could walk or dance for many hours and I was never tired.

Life changes all the time. I cannot tell which part of my life was better. Of course, school is not such a pleasure like parties every single night, but it is more important for my future. I know that now the best time to do something is during the day. I have to study and to exercise, so of course, days are a better time to do this. On the other hand, I miss my friends and all the parties we had. I cannot wait until December when I will go home for a winter break. Probably "the best" time will change again.

– Viola Madej (532 words)

Analysis of Sample Seven:

Sample Seven has as its hook, a definition set apart, that the writer ties in to the first sentence of the essay. A two-part thesis is the last sentence of the introduction. The body paragraphs are balanced in length. In the first body paragraph, the writer moves in time from high school days to college days and shows appropriate changes in verb tense. The second body paragraph, set in the past, has one lapse in correct verb tense. The conclusion demonstrates a "So What?" ending, as the student begins the ending with a philosophical comment.

Sample Eight – Example

Topic: What kinds of movies do you like and why?

Having started with short silent films of only a few minutes in length, the cinema has extended to a variety of extraordinary movies today. There are some kinds of movies that can really get and keep my attention such as suspense and romance movies.

I really enjoy watching suspense movies that keep my attention from the beginning of the movie until the word "End." A good movie is like a good book that as soon as you start, you can't be interrupted until you finish it. For example, *Silence of the Lamb* is one of the best movies I have ever seen because I didn't guess who the killer was after ten minutes of watching like most of the other movies. Afraid to miss any detail that could help me guess the killer, I could not walk away from the movie for even one second. I like to forget life and reality for a few hours and to be in a complete fantasy for awhile. Another suspense movie that I liked was *Seven* with Brad Pitt who is investigating a serial killer. It was highly improbable to guess who the killer is.

After having lost all hope of being in love again, she saw him, and they knew that that was it. They knew that they were born for each other. I love these romantic movies because they give me a moment of dream, of hope that some day it is going to happen to me. Romance is so beautiful and so sad at the same time, and I like that because love without suffering is too boring. For example, *The Legends of The Fall* is so romantic that I saw it more than four times, and because all of their love was impossible, it was so romantic and interesting. Indeed, the best movie I liked was *Don Juan*, the lover of every woman on earth. For the short time of the movie, I saw myself as a woman and being loved for that. Moreover, I really enjoy the stories in which people are forbidden from enjoying their love and because of that, they get to know its real importance. I like the movies where love is the winner at the end, as in *Dirty Dancing*, where after hard and beautiful times, the love of Patrick Swayze and Jennifer Grey finally won.

Today, cinema and movies are very important in everyone's life. Of course, nowadays there are all kinds of movies, and people develop their preferences with time. In my case, I really love all kinds of movies, but I most enjoy suspense and romance movies. A good movie can let me forget who I am or what my life is, and I would just live the character's life and would learn so much from his or her experience. Even though it is not always reality and that's what makes it have its charm, I like to watch a movie to relax and forget everything.

–Iman Foufa (500 words)

Analysis of Sample Eight:

Sample Eight, a full-developed and refined essay of five hundred words, has a short 2-sentence introduction and a clear thesis. The body paragraphs are full of lively detail and are of approximately equal length. In particular, body paragraph 2 with its discussion of three examples shows the maturity of the student's writing ability with examples that are developed, not superficially mentioned. Sentences are long and of sufficient syntactic complexity, many of them using complex structures with adverb clauses and participle phrases. The ending is thoughtful, with a "So What?" conclusion and a restatement.

Sample Nine – Contrast Essay

Topic: *Contrast your ideas about living at home with the ideas your parents have about living at home.*

Many of us, at some time in our lives, while living without parents, have made them upset about our behavior. It is really hard to tell why children feel the need to rebel against their parents. These rebellious ideas make our parents feel disappointed. Even today when children are still living with their parents, they always have some ideas with which their parents disagree. For my family, my parents and I have many different ideas, but I think eating Vietnamese food, watching American movies, and dressing like Americans are the chief differences between my parents and me.

Because my parents grew up and lived in Vietnam for more than forty years, they always think only Vietnamese food is the best. They cannot live without it. At home they cook Vietnamese food all the time for us to eat. In the morning, afternoon, and evening I have to eat what they cook, but I do not enjoy Vietnamese food at all. I only like American food because I went to high school in the United States, where they serve American food everyday. Now I have grown to enjoy hamburgers, pizzas, and hot dogs; in fact, I cannot live without American food. Every time I order pizza or a Big Mac, my parents yell at me and tell me not to bring it home for them to see.

In addition, I love to watch American action movies. I used to go to Blockbuster to rent some action movies every week, but because my parents did not like me to watch those kind of movies, I only watched them when they were not at home. My parents say, if I watch too many American action movies, I will learn to fight and do all kinds of bad things they portray in the movies. But I think each person has his or her own interest. Even though some people in the society have done many violent and socially questionable acts depicted in films, it does not mean that I will do what people do.

Furthermore, my parents still keep in mind the old traditional Vietnamese culture. They do not like to see their children dress like Americans and forget about Vietnamese culture. They prefer me to wear something which looks Vietnamese. They tell me that because I am Vietnamese, I should make myself look like I am Vietnamese. Even though we are living in America, they still do not want me to dress like an American. On the other hand, I feel that if I am living in a different culture, and I should adapt to the culture in which I live. Though I come from Vietnam, I still need to assimilate into American culture if I expect to thrive here.

In the end, my parents and I have many different ideas, but the ideas that I have listed above are the most important. These ideas make us have a hard time to understand each other. Therefore, I think because of living in a different culture, young people's ideas change while old people's do not.

– Chanh N. Lam (510 words)

Sample Ten – Past Narrative Essay

Topic: What has been the worst job or the best job that you have ever had? What did you do? What are some of the dissatisfying or satisfying things that happened in that job? What did you learn?

During summer vacation twelve years ago while I was in high school in Italy, I decided with my friends to go on vacation in August. Our destination was the Adriatic sea, but to go there I needed money. I did not want to ask my parents for it, so I decided to go around my town to find a temporary job for the month of July. It did not matter to me what kind of job it was. The important thing was to make enough cash to afford my trip. I started searching for a job which turned out to be the worst job I ever had. It was the worst for three reasons, – the encounter with the boss, the actual job, and the overall experience.

After two days of searching, I landed in a factory not too far from my house. I remember a skinny man who was outside the building doing something. I asked him if I could talk with the boss. He said, "I'm the boss." So I asked him if he needed me for a temporary job, and how much he wanted to pay me for it per hour. He answered me 3,000 lira (that is about $2.00 per hour). That number was very important to do my budget. After our verbal agreement, I decided to accept that job which consisted of ironing stockings.

The day after the interview, I was ready to jump in the real world. I was a little worried because I had never worked before, but also curious about it. I arrived there on time at 8:00 A.M. The boss assigned me a place where I had to work from that day to the end of July. As I said before, I had to iron stockings. There was an iron which was set on a table that had the shape of a woman's legs. These woman's legs were made of steel, and they were upside down. To iron stockings, I had to put them on it. As the days passed, I became as fast as the other workers were.

There were about twenty girls that did that job for over two years. They had spent over two years of their lives in a gray building with two big windows. During our breaks, I had the opportunity to meet them and to talk with them.

In our conversations, I found out that not only most of them were underinsured, but also that they were paid less than me. At that point I realized that there was something not quite right. I started to notice many irregularities, and I explained them to the workers. Unfortunately, my words were misunderstood by everyone, and on pay day, the boss called me and gave me my check for a lower amount than I expected. Clearly our verbal agreement for him was not important. I was very disappointed about my experience, but because I fought for my rights, I eventually received the correct amount.

I will always remember that day and that work experience for the rest of my life not only because that job turned out to be the worst job I ever had, but also because what I faced was dissatisfaction. What I learned from this experience is that to work is hard. It can be much harder than the actual work if there is an untrustworthy boss who makes the work experience unpleasant.

– Manuela Saramondi (592 words)

Sample Eleven – Argumentative Essay

Topic: *If you were running for the Student Government Office, what are the issues that you would propose as changes?*

It was a dull and gray Saturday afternoon. When I got on the bus, it began to drizzle, causing fog to slowly creep on the window panes of the bus. Unfortunately, the bus seats were all occupied, so I stood in the aisle. Every twist and turn of the rectangular vehicle threw me here and there on other people. After the second stop the bus made, I tried to see my own stop, but with no avail. Luckily enough, someone else had hit the bell, so I thankfully got off the bus. Then a forceful surge of water hit me. It was so unexpected that I nearly fell down onto the muddy pavement. A long struggle with the torrential rain followed, and after being drenched with a pool of water on the curb by a passing car, I managed to get into the library with a soaking shirt and wet pants. However, my series of misfortunes had not yet ended. When I got to the Computer Lab, the Lab assistant asked me to wait outside, as all the computers were occupied. After waiting for seven minutes suddenly, everyone was leaving the Lab. As I entered the Lab, the lab assistant told me that it was closed. It was then that I discovered that the access hours to the Computer Lab were restricted to fewer hours on the weekends. This brings me to two points that I would like to change if I were running for Student Government Office including the use of the Computer Lab and the problems with parking decals.

The Computer Lab is a top priority to students of DeKalb College. A $25 technology fee is paid by every student of DeKalb College to support the upkeep of this Lab as well as its utilities. Thus the Lab hours of operation should cover a time span fairly suitable to all. Students usually use the Lab during morning hours through the afternoon until about five p.m. During the weekends, the Lab ought to be open during these hours as well, to help those people who do not have a personal computer at home and to make full use of the Lab. The numbers of computers is also a fact to be considered. There are 48 computers in the Lab, and the population of the school is increasing every quarter. The number of people on the waiting list in the Lab sometimes exceeds twenty, which is almost half the number of computers in the Lab itself. This means that about half of the total numbers of computers need to be installed in the lab to ensure a better level of efficiency.

Although the use of the Computer Lab is important, arriving at the school campus on time is equally essential. As far as driving is concerned, there is always the incurable disease of traffic jams on the freeway. A soothing remedy to this disease was parking decals. Normally, each student enrolled in DeKalb College has paid a $5 parking fee, which if not used would surely be a great waste of money and an easy profit for the school. Yet many complaints have come up during the course of the quarter, indicating that the decals are not being given out as earlier stated by the Protective Services department of the college. Many students have trouble parking in the parking lots, and consequently, destabilized students overcrowd the visitors' parking lots. Therefore, decals need to be issued on time to enhance the flow of traffic in and out of the school.

It is clear that if these facts are regarded, the result will be highly positive. As computers are very essential for the developing student, not only will the grades in assignments, projects, and tests increase, but also the general grade point average of students will increase. This will raise the reputation of the college across the state, and eventually the nation. The parking situation in the college will also be of help to the students attending the college, as the student age range is very wide. This will bring more credit to the citizens attending DeKalb College, as they will be able to attend the right place for a sound education.

– Ghamoti Anye Angwafo (720 words)

Sample Twelve – A Literary Paper on "Las Papas"

Potatoes: The Importance of National Identity

Julio Ortega is a twentieth century writer and is originally from Peru. In his story "Las Papas," he tells the story of a man who lives with his son and likes to cook. The character tries to teach Peruvian identity to his son through cooking the Peruvian dishes the way his father used to do. Ortega tells us the man discovers how important national identity is.

The man is forty years old and lives with his six year old son. He likes to cook and he tries to learn something from cooking. Ortega writes: "If he tried to cook something it passed the time, and he also amused himself with the child's curiosity" (173). This passage explains that the man tries to teach his son Peruvian identity using not books but experience. Also the man realized that he did not know anything about his country through his cooking of potatoes.

Ortega uses potatoes as a symbol of how important national identity is. The man realizes that national identity is important. He discovers this by being with his son and remembering when he was young. At a young age, he did not care about national identity. Ortega explains this: "For a long time he had avoided eating them [potatoes]. Even their name seemed unpleasant to him, papas" (172). Although his father tried to tell him about Peruvian identity, he refused to listen. He realizes that young people don't care about their national identities but gradually do care when they become older. The potato is a symbol of his discovery of the importance of identity. "It was as if he discovered one of the lost varieties of the Andean potato: the one that belonged to him, ..." (173). Now the man wants to learn more about his country.

In brief, the man learned that identity is very important and should keep teaching the next generations. Now he cares about his nationality and he is nostalgic when he realized what he had done to his father. His resolution is his discovery of identity and he tries to stand by his national identity in the United States. As a resolution, he plants the potato that he found in his kitchen. His son is watching and laughing because he is too young to understand what identity is; however, the son will know when he grows up.

– Miwa Maejima (387 words)

Primary source: Julio Ortega, "Las Papas" in *The International Story.* Ed. Ruth Spack. St. Martin's Press. New York . 1994. (Pages 171-175).

Section Five:
Writing Topics and Assignments

Composition Topics for Timed Writing
Self-Evaluation Exercise
Writing a Description of Place
Writing a Description of a Person
Writing a Comparison/Contrast Essay

Composition Topics for Timed Writing Practice

Below is a list of typical topics for timed writing. Familiarize yourself with the topics. Use this list to practice writing under pressure.

Conditionals

1. If you could improve one thing about the world, what would it be and why?

2. If you could have a household robot, what jobs would you program it for?

3. If you could spend the day with someone from your past, who would it be and why?

4. If your college received a substantial donation for either computers for the computer lab or books for the library, which would you choose and why?

Comparison/Contrast

1. Contrast living in a large city to living in a small town.

2. Contrast yourself with another member of your family.

3. Contrast your two favorite TV shows or movies.

4. Contrast a novel that you have read with the film of the same novel.

Cause and Effect

1. If you were a college professor, what would cause you to expel a student from your class?

2. What are some causes for divorce in the United States?

3. What are some effects of too much television watching?

Expository

1. Write about a public figure, alive or dead, whom you admire.

2. In what ways does a college education change you for the rest of your life?

3. What makes one college class more enjoyable than another?

4. What has been the best piece of advice you ever received?

5. Write about a good friendship that you have had with someone from another country.

6. Why do students return to college after many years in the work world?

Self Evaluation: Analyzing and Writing About Your Past Writing

Out of Class Writing Project

Discussion of the Project: For this paper, you will be investigating your own writing ability from your former ESL writing class. The two questions you want to ask yourself and your former ESL teacher are:

1. **What are my strengths in writing English?**
2. **What are my specific problem areas in writing English?**

As soon as possible, you are to contact your former ESL teacher and make an appointment to discuss your past compositions, in particular your final writing. Let your former teacher know that this appointment is part of an assignment. After your face to face talk (where you should take notes and look at your final writing), you should have some specific information. You should get some examples from your papers of the kinds of errors that you made. In addition, you should come away with some concrete knowledge of what you are doing right and what you need to focus on now.

Writing the Paper: After taking notes from the interview, begin thinking of a thesis for this paper and begin organizing your notes into some logical form. This could easily be divided into a four paragraph essay with an introduction, two body paragraphs (one mentioning the strengths and the other mentioning the problem areas), and a conclusion. Be sure to edit your paper when you have finished. This essay can be used as a discussion focus with your teacher as well as a way to set goals for yourself for the new class.

Guidelines for analyzing your own essay:

Writing
     introduction with a clear thesis
     body paragraphs with support and/or developed ideas
     conclusion
     cohesion and non-repetitive progression of ideas
     range of vocabulary
     smooth flow
     meets minimum word length (if part of criteria)

Grammar
     sentence variety
     correct verb usage
     lacks agreement and number errors
     correct article use
     correct use of word forms
     correct use of punctuation
     absence of non-English structures and non-idiomatic use of language

Writing Assignment: Writing a Description of Place

Instructions: *Go to a place on campus and write a description of it.*

When you write a description, you need to focus on two aspects. First, you need to focus on an overall impression or feeling that a place gives you and convey that impression to the reader. Pick out details that support your feelings about the place. For example, if the place makes you sad, look around for the colors, shapes, and textures that cause that feeling and describe them.

Second, you need to organize your details according to some pattern. Present what you see to the reader with a recognized spatial organization. Use one of the following patterns to present the details which best describe the place where you are. It is a good idea to map out the major features of the place and organize them in one of the patterns below.

Left to right or right to left   Top to bottom or bottom to top

← *you*   Away from you or close toward you → *you*

Your description is successful if you can create a vivid picture for the reader, a place where the reader sees, hears, feels, and smells what you do. That is communication and good writing. Try to see if you can do it!

Go to the place. Look around. Think about how this place makes you feel. Take notes and draw a map. Write the composition. Reread it. Change it. Finally, edit it applying the grammar rules that we have studied in class. This is a fun assignment. Be imaginative. Enjoy writing.

Vocabulary that will help you:

Shapes	Textures	Materials	Colors
square	rough	brick	beige
rectangular	smooth	marble	brick-colored
round	silky	concrete	winter brown
oval	uneven	glass and glass bricks	emerald green
triangular		asphalt	mauve
		leather	ivory
		carpet	

Landscape and plants	Feelings	
maple trees	melancholy	
bedding plants	surprised	**Miscellaneous**
pansies	depressed	winding staircase
shrubs	hassled	fountain
crape myrtles	excited	bleachers
artificial plants	elated	asymmetrical
cherry trees	homesick	benches
oak trees	relaxed	planters
	spiritual	
	bored	

Writing Assignment: Writing a Description of a Person

Instructions: *Choose a person to write about. This person should be someone that you see every day and have positive feelings about. Filling out the worksheet below will help you get started. After you have gathered some preliminary notes, figure out an organizing principle for the essay before beginning your paper. Descriptions are not easy to write. Through the writing process, you will often gain a new look a person who is close to you.*

Your relationship to the person: _____

A physical description of the person: _____

A description of the person's general mood and temperament: _____

What is this person's background (nationality, education, religion)? _____

Generally, what does this person do every day? _____

Whom does he/she lives with? _____

How much does this person talk and to whom? _____

What was your last long conversation with this person? _____

Describe your feelings towards this person. _____

How does this person feel about you? _____

What do you like best about this person? _____

What are some things that you don't like about this person? _____

What are his/her goals? _____

Describe some of the worries, anxieties of this person. _____

Where do you think this person will be in five years?_____

What is your dominant impression of this person? _____

Writing a Comparison/Contrast Essay

Much of what we do in our daily lives is comparison shopping. We review the want ads to search out the best used car for sale; we pick out the right kind of spaghetti sauce in the grocery store; we choose a college that will suit our needs. Big decisions, small decisions – we constantly compare and contrast.

Comparison and contrast writing is used as a means of presenting ideas on a variety of topics. Frequently required by history, political science, psychology, sociology, and literature professors, comparison and contrast, however, is not an end in itself; this mode is a way for writers to discover and to explore topics. Two basic organizational patterns, or some combination of them, are followed, and the writer chooses the one pattern that best suits his/her topic and audience. One pattern is the **"All of one, all of the other"** in which one idea is totally described, and then the other is similarly described. The other common pattern is the **"Point-by-Point"** in which the writer clearly and directly notes the contrast. Examine the differences in outline formats for papers stemming from the same thesis.

Thesis: Practices and beliefs in regards to formality in class and question asking in class differ in university classrooms in Asian countries and in the U.S.

"All of One, All of the Other"	"Point-by-Point"
I. In Asian Countries	I. Formality in Class
A. Formality in Class	A. In Asian Countries
B. Question Asking in Class	B. In the U.S.
II. In the United States	II. Question Asking in Class
A. Formality in Class	A. In Asian Countries
B. Question Asking in Class	B. In the U.S.

Read Sample Nine that has a "point-by-point" pattern. Write an essay on one of the following topics. Make sure that your bases for contrast are not just surface contrasts. Use this assignment to explore some new relationships between ideas or people.

Topic 1: Contrast living at home with your family versus living alone or with a friend.

Topic 2: Contrast two members of your family.

Topic 3: Contrast two different ESL programs that you have attended.

Topic 4: Contrast the grammar of your native language with the grammar structure of English. (You may want to look at the chart of languages in the introduction of this book.)